W0221494

Gute Noten in ENGLISCH

Klasse 7

Susan Bollinger
Angela Drude-Moss

ullmann medien um

Zeichnungen: Sabine Völkers, Berlin
Layout: Cordula Schaaf, München
Umschlagabbildung: Monkey Business Images, shutterstock
Umschlaggestaltung: Stefanie Brüssel, Potsdam

www.ullmannmedien.com
© Genehmigte Sonderausgabe für Ullmann Medien GmbH, Birkenstraße 10, D-14469 Potsdam

Das Werk und seine Teile sind urheberrechtlich geschützt. Jede Verwertung in anderen als den gesetzlich zugelassenen Fällen bedarf daher der vorherigen schriftlichen Einwilligung des Verlages.

Gesamtherstellung: Ullmann Medien GmbH, Potsdam

ISBN 978-3-7415-0444-0

Inhalt

1 Zeiten

2 Modale Hilfsverben

3 Pronomen

4 Passiv

5 Indirekte Rede

6 Satzformen

7 Textverständnis

8 Wortschatz und Situationen

Lösungen

★ Dieses Sternchen markiert Übungen und Regeln, die etwas anspruchsvoller sind oder nicht überall verlangt werden. Wenn du ganz sicher bist, dass du sie nicht brauchst, kannst du sie überspringen. Ansonsten gilt: Stell dich der Herausforderung!

1 Zeiten

The Grüner family consists of Mr and Mrs Grüner and their two children, Julia and Stefan. They are originally from Cologne, but now live in Osnabrück. Julia is fifteen years old and has been learning English for six years now. She has an English pen-friend, Katie Johnson, who lives in Canterbury. Julia visited Katie two years ago, but hopes very much to be able to visit her again in the summer holidays and maybe take her brother Stefan with her as well, as he has been getting poor grades in English at school.

1.1 *Revision*: *Simple Present, Present Perfect, Simple Past* und *Past Progressive*

Alles klar?! ***Simple Present*** **– eine Zeitform, mit der du über die Gegenwart sprichst**

*Julia **goes** to school by bike every day.*

*The school **is** near her home.*

*She **lives** in Osnabrück.*

*She **often eats** cornflakes in the morning.*

Das *simple present* wird verwendet:

- für regelmäßige und gewohnheitsmäßige Handlungen,
- bei Tatsachenbeschreibungen,
- bei Zustandsverben.

Signalwörter: *always, often, sometimes, never, every week, on Fridays*

Alles klar?! ***Simple Past*** **– eine Zeitform, mit der du über die Vergangenheit sprichst**

*Last year she **had** a nice holiday in a holiday camp at the seaside near her home.*

Das *simple past* wird verwendet:

- für abgeschlossene Ereignisse in der Vergangenheit.

Signalwörter: *yesterday, last week, four years ago*

Alles klar?! ***Present Perfect*** **– eine Zeitform, die eine Verbindung von der Vergangenheit zur Gegenwart herstellt**

*Julia **has learned** English for six years.*

*The Grüners **have** just **talked** about Julia's trip to England.*

*Julia **has made** a lot of plans for her trip.*

*Julia **has** already **been** on a holiday without her family.*

Das *present perfect* wird verwendet:

- für Ereignisse, die in der Vergangenheit anfingen und in der Gegenwart andauern,
- für Ereignisse, die gerade abgeschlossen wurden,
- für Ereignisse, die abgeschlossen sind, aber Auswirkung auf die Gegenwart haben,
- für Ereignisse, die in der Vergangenheit stattfanden, ohne Zeitangabe.

Signalwörter: *just, not yet, up to now, already, since* + Zeitpunkt, *for* + Zeitraum, *ever, so far, never, today, this morning/week* (wenn dieser Zeitraum noch nicht vorbei ist)

Übung 1 **Setze die Verben in die richtige Form: *simple present/present perfect*.**

1. The Grüners .... (live) in Osnabrück.
2. They .... (live) there for six years.
3. Julia usually .... (go) to school by bike.
4. The cycle ride to school .... (take) 20 minutes.
5. Today her father .... (take) her by car.
6. This morning she .... (arrive) in school early.

Übung 2 **Markiere die richtige Verbform.**

1. Before they moved to Osnabrück, the Grüners have lived/lived in Cologne.
2. Yesterday Thomas has broken/broke his leg.
3. Mark is sad, because he has lost/lost his football.
4. Katie has sent/sent Julia a present for her birthday last week.
5. Mandy has just finished/just finished her homework.
6. Jan has bought/bought a new computer game on the way home from school.

Übung 3 ★ **Setze die Verben in die richtige Form.**

Julia .... (be) 16 years old and her brother Stefan, who .... (be) 13 years old, both .... (live) with their parents in Osnabrück. They .... both .... (attend) the local grammar school since they .... (be) ten years old. Stefan .... (not, like) foreign languages, but Julia .... (have) an English penfriend for three years. Two years ago she .... (visit) her friend Katie in Canterbury. She .... (enjoy) herself very much and .... (hope) to return soon. Stefan .... (never, be) abroad; he .... (prefer) to spend his holidays camping with friends. While Julia .... (visit) Katie, Stefan .... (have) a holiday beside a lake in Bavaria. Julia .... (try) to send an email to Katie every week and Katie .... (always, reply) immediately. They .... (plan) to spend another holiday together when they .... (pass) their tests at the end of the school year.

Lösungen Seite 98

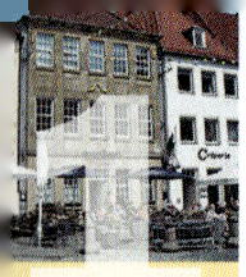

Alles klar?! ***Past Progressive*** **– eine Zeitform, mit der man über einen Zeitraum in der Vergangenheit spricht**

past progressive	***simple past***
Julia ***was writing*** *an email to the Johnsons*	*when the Johnsons called.*

Handlung in der Vergangenheit, die während eines bestimmten **Zeitraums** abläuft, sie bildet oft den „Hintergrund“ für ein Ereignis in der Vergangenheit.	Ereignis in der Vergangenheit

- Bei kurz aufeinanderfolgenden Ereignissen in der Vergangenheit wird nur *simple past* verwendet.
- Bei mehreren gleichzeitigen Ereignissen kann auch *past progressive* verwendet werden.
- Auch wenn du Verlauf und Länge einer Handlung oder eines Vorgangs in der Vergangenheit besonders betonen möchtest, verwendest du *past progressive*.

Übung 4 ***Simple past or past progressive*****? Markiere die richtige Verbform (es können auch beide Formen richtig sein).**

1. What was Julia doing/did Julia do when Stefan entered/was entering the room?
2. Julia finished/was finishing her letter, then she was doing/did her homework.
3. While Stefan was watching/watched TV, Julia was phoning/phoned Mary.
4. Stefan and his friends played/were playing football when it started/was starting to rain.
5. Stefan picked/was picking up the ball and ran/was running home as quickly as possible.
6. Stefan and Julia ate/were eating their supper before they went/were going to the cinema.

Lösungen Seite 98

1.2 Present Perfect Progressive

Alles klar?! ***Present Perfect Progressive***

Julia ***has been thinking*** *about her trip to England all day.*

Das *present perfect progressive* wird gebildet:

- mit dem Hilfsverb *have:*
  Singular: *I have, you have, he/she/it has*
  Plural: *we have, you have, they have*

  und
- dem ***past participle*** (Partizip Perfekt) von *to be: been*

  und
- der ***-ing*-Form** (= Grundform des Verbs + *-ing*, z. B. *think + -ing*).

Julia has noted down the questions she wants to ask.

Julia ***has been writing*** *an email all morning.*

Das *present perfect progressive* wird verwendet:

Das *present perfect simple* betont das Ergebnis einer Handlung.

Das *present perfect progressive* betont das Andauern einer Handlung.

Signalwörter: *all day, all night, since, for, how long*

Übung 1 **Setze die richtige Form des Verbs ein: *present perfect/present perfect progressive.***

1. Stefan .... (never, be) to England.
2. Julia .... (write) a letter to her penfriend all morning.
3. Mother .... (prepare) the lunch, but Julia .... (not, set) the table.
4. Stefan .... (camp) in Bavaria since last Tuesday.
5. Julia and Stefan .... (live) in Osnabrück for six years.
6. Julia .... (learn) English for four years.

Tipp

Wenn du dir überlegst, wie das *present progressive* und das *present perfect* gebildet werden, kannst du dir die Bildung des *present perfect progressive* selbst herleiten.

Lösungen Seite 98

Übung 2 ★ **Setze die richtige Form des Verbs ein: *simple present/present perfect/ present perfect progressive/simple past/past progressive.***

Every summer for the past five years Julia and Stefan's parents, Mr and Mrs Grüner, ... (have) a barbecue in their garden for friends and neighbours. Last year, just when everyone .... (have) a good time, it .... (start) to rain heavily. All the guests .... (rush) inside, but Julia and Stefan .... (try) to carry as much indoors as they .... (can). While Stefan .... (pick) up all the glasses and dishes, Julia .... (take) plates of food into the kitchen. When no one .... (look), the family dog, Benno, ... (eat) a large number of sausages. This year the Grüner family .... (decide) to hire a large tent. They .... (want) to stay dry however bad the weather .... (be), and they also .... (hope) that Benno, who without doubt .... (dream) of sausages ever since, will not eat as many as last year.

Lösungen Seite 99

1.3 *Past Perfect/Past Perfect Progressive*

Alles klar?! ***Past Perfect*** **– eine Zeitform, mit der du über die Zeit vor der Vergangenheit sprichst.**

Das *past perfect* wird gebildet:

Julia ***had finished*** *her letter before she went to school.*	• mit der Vergangenheitsform von *to have = had* und dem Partizip Perfekt.

Das *past perfect* wird verwendet:

Julia ***had*** *already* ***finished*** *her letter before she went to school.*

Ereignis **vor** einem Zeitpunkt der Vergangenheit = *1st action*

Ereignis in der Vergangenheit = *2nd action*

Für Ereignisse, die noch vor einem Zeitpunkt in der Vergangenheit *(simple past)* stattfanden.

Signalwörter: *after, before, as soon as, when*

Merke

Zur Erinnerung: Die regelmäßige Form des Partizip Perfekts wird gebildet, indem du an den Infinitiv *-ed* anhängst: *finished, listened, phoned, worked, …*

Die unregelmäßige Form musst du lernen: *drunk, eaten, seen, read …* Es ist jeweils die dritte Form in der Liste der unregelmäßigen Verben (vgl. Seite 124 ff.). Wenn du einzelne Formen vergessen hast, solltest du die Liste noch einmal wiederholen.

Übung 1 **Bilde Sätze anhand der Informationen in der Tabelle.**

	1st action	2nd action
Stefan	play tennis	have a shower
The guests	arrive	switch on all the lights
Julia	write a letter	go to the post-box
The lightning	strike the house	catch fire
Benno	finish all the sausages	fall asleep
The teacher	write the questions	start work

1. After Stefan ………………………………………………, he ………………………………………………….
2. When the guests ……………………………………, Mr Grüner ……………………………………………….
3. As soon as Julia ……………………………………………, she …………………………………………….
4. After the lightning …………………………………………, it ………………………………………………….
5. Before Benno ……………………………………………, he ……………………………………………….
6. As soon as the teacher ……………………………………, the pupils …………………………………….

Alles klar?! ***Past Perfect Progressive***

Das *past perfect progressive* wird gebildet:

*Julia was cold; she **had been waiting** at the bus stop for 20 minutes.*

- wie das *present perfect progressive*, wobei das Hilfsverb *have* in der Vergangenheit steht.

Das *past perfect progressive* wird verwendet:

*Julia was cold; she **had been waiting** at the bus stop for 20 minutes.*

- für Handlungen, die (fast) bis zu einem bestimmten Zeitpunkt in der Vergangenheit *(past tense)* angedauert haben,
- mit Tätigkeitsverben, wenn die Dauer betont wird.

Signalwörter: *after, for, since, how long?*

Lösungen Seite 99

Übung 2 **Setze die Verben in *past perfect* oder *past perfect progressive*.**

1. When the train finally drew into the station, the passengers .... (wait) for twenty minutes.
2. Benno .... (already, eat) seven sausages when the twins found him under the table.
3. The Grüners .... (always, invite) friends to a party in their house, but last year they had a barbecue in the garden.
4. Mr Grüner .... (worry) for some time about the weather and decided to hire a tent.
5. When Julia .... (learn) English for three years, she had the chance of getting an English penfriend.
6. Stefan .... (never, want) to learn a foreign language, but he quite liked English.

Übung 3 **Verbinde die Satzhälften zu sinnvollen Sätzen.**

1. *Stefan had been playing tennis for two hours …*	a) one hour after Mrs Grüner had ordered the taxi.
2. *The doorbell finally rang …*	b) after they had been laughing and shouting all morning.
3. *Katie was late for her riding lesson …*	c) they moved to Osnabrück.
4. *Ben's knee hurt …*	d) when rain stopped play.
5. *After they had been living in Cologne for eight years …*	e) because she had been talking on the phone for hours.
6. *The teacher gave the class extra work …*	f) after he had fallen down on the football pitch.

Lösungen Seite 99

1.4 *Future*

Alles klar?! **Revision: *Expressing Future Time***

***will*-future**	1. *Julia's school holidays* ***will start*** *next month.* 2. *Her mum thinks she* ***will like*** *her holidays in Britain.* 3. *Are you thirsty? – I'****ll get*** *you a drink.*	1. zukünftige Ereignisse, die man nicht beeinflussen kann. 2. Vermutungen, Hoffnungen, Voraussagen 3. spontane Entscheidungen für die Zukunft
***going-to*-future**	1. *Julia* ***is going to spend*** *her next holiday in Britain.* 2. *Look at those grey clouds. It'****s going to rain****.*	1. feste Vorhaben, Pläne und Absichten 2. Voraussagen über Ereignisse, die sich schon anbahnen und mit großer Sicherheit eintreten werden
simple present	*Julia's train* ***leaves*** *at 9 o'clock.*	Zeitplan, Fahrplan
present progressive	*She* ***is spending*** *her summer holiday in Britain this year. Her parents have already booked the tickets.*	feste Vereinbarungen
future progressive	1. *Next month* ***she'll be talking*** *English with the Johnsons.* 2. ***Will*** *the Johnsons* ***be having*** *a barbecue when Julia is there?*	1. für Handlungen von begrenzter Dauer, die zu einem bestimmten zukünftigen Zeitpunkt stattfinden 2. ein Ereignis, das man als gegeben ansieht

Lösungen Seite 100

Übung 1 ***Will* oder *going to*? Markiere die richtige Form.**

1. The carnival procession is going to/will take place next week.
2. My daughter is going to/will be a princess in the procession.
3. Hundreds of people are going to/will cheer as the procession goes past.
4. I am sure they are going to/will enjoy themselves.
5. It's already late, I am going to/will find us a place with a good view of the procession.
6. With the streets so full of people you are going to/will find it difficult to get to the station.

Übung 2 **Bilde Sätze, indem du die richtige Futurform einsetzt.**

1. The Grüners/have/a party tonight. It/start/at 6 pm.

....

2. I am sure that we/have/a good view of the procession from here.

....

3. What/do/he/this time tomorrow?

....

4. Hurry up! It is after 6 o'clock/and/we/be/late.

....

5. The procession/leave/the town hall at 2 pm.

....

Lösungen Seite 100

Abschlusstest (30 Minuten)

Aufgabe 1 **Vervollständige die Sätze, indem du *simple present, simple past* oder *present perfect* einsetzt.**

1. Stefan .... (like) camping since he .... (be) six.
2. Stefan .... (want) to go camping with his friend Jan in the Easter holidays.
3. Jan .... (never, be) camping before.
4. Stefan .... (tell) him what fun camping .... (be).
5. Last time Stefan and his friends .... (take) their bikes with them.
6. Jan's parents .... (allow) him to go camping with Stefan and his friends.

Punkte: ☐ von 8

Aufgabe 2 **Setze die Verben in die richtige Form, entweder *simple past* oder *past progressive*.**

1. While the other boys .... (put up) the tent, Stefan and Thomas .... (fetch) water from the nearby farm.
2. When Stefan and Thomas .... (return) to the camp, the others .... (unpack) the food.
3. While the water .... (boil), everyone .... (help) to prepare the meal.
4. They .... (eat) their meal when it .... (start) raining.
5. When the rain .... (stop), the boys .... (wash) the dishes and then .... (play) a game of football.
6. While they .... (play) football, the farmer .... (arrive) with some fresh eggs.

Punkte: ☐ von 13

Lösungen Seite 100

Aufgabe 3 **Markiere die richtige Form: *present perfect* oder *present perfect progressive*. Manchmal sind beide Verbformen möglich.**

1. Katie has been learning/has learnt German for four years.
2. She has just written/has just been writing a long letter to Julia about her trip to Folkestone.
3. Has Jan gone/Has Jan been going to school today?
4. Stefan has done/has been doing his homework, but Julia has been helping/has helped their mother.
5. Stefan and Jan have spent/have been spending a week at the camp.
6. Mr Grüner has cleaned/has been cleaning the barbecue all morning.

Punkte: ☐ von 7

Aufgabe 4 **Bilde Sätze mit den unterstrichenen Verben in *simple past*, *past perfect* oder *past perfect progressive*.**

1. The boys/camp/for a week/when their parents/come/to fetch them.

....

2. How long/wait/you/for her when she/phone/you?

....

3. Thomas/never/like English/until he/spend/a holiday in London.

....

4. Jan/play/computer games for hours/when his mother/arrive/home from work.

....

5. When she/be/a child/Katie/learn/the piano.

....

6. Ever since she/be/six years old/Katie/want/to have a horse.

....

Punkte: ☐ von 12

Lösungen Seite 100/101

Aufgabe 5 **Future forms: Markiere die richtige Form des Verbs.**

1. Look at the lovely blue sky, it will/is going to be a fine day.
2. Julia is planning/will plan to visit Katie next year.
3. The bus to Canterbury leaves/is going to leave at 6 pm.
4. When she has finished her homework, Julia is writing/will write to Katie.
5. When I leave school, I will become/am going to become a teacher.
6. Next year Julia is going to visit/will be visiting Katie.

Punkte: ☐ von 6

Aufgabe 6 **Setze die richtige Verbform in die Lücken:**
simple present/present progressive; simple past/past progressive; present perfect/ present perfect progressive; past perfect/past perfect progressive or future forms.

On Julia's first visit to England two years ago, she .... (spend) all the time with Katie in Canterbury. While she .... (be) there, they .... (discuss) her next visit. Now Julia .... (make) definite plans. She .... (hope) to see more of the country this time. She .... (look) at travel brochures and .... (decide) which places she .... (want) to see. She .... (leave) for Britain at the end of term and .... (spend) four weeks with Katie. They .... (visit) London, of course, but Julia .... (also, plan) a trip to other parts of the UK. She .... (hope) to visit Northern Ireland, but .... (find out) that there .... (not, be) enough time. She .... (definitely, visit) York and Edinburgh. This .... (mean) that she .... (see) at least two of the countries of the UK.

Punkte: ☐ von 18

Punkte: ☐ von 64

51–64: Bravo! Du weißt über die Zeiten schon gut Bescheid.
31–50: Teilweise bist du sicher, teilweise noch nicht. Bearbeite noch einmal die Übungen, in denen du beim ersten Mal viele Fehler hattest.
0–30: Leider ist dir noch zu vieles unklar. Arbeite das Kapitel noch einmal durch.

Lösungen Seite 101

2

Modale Hilfsverben

Julia is planning her next trip to Britain. She will stay with Katie in Canterbury for a short while, but then they will try to visit as many places as possible in England and Scotland. Stefan is going as well because he needs to practise his English. At the moment, however, he is looking forward only to the Edinburgh Tattoo because he finds the sound of the bagpipes fascinating.

2.1 Modale Hilfsverben *can/could/to be able to/ to be allowed to*

Alles klar?! ***Can – could – to be able to – to be allowed to***

	***Can* kann Folgendes ausdrücken:**
*Julia **can speak** English quite well.*	• körperliche und geistige Fähigkeiten eines Menschen
*You **can't take** too many things with you.*	• eine Erlaubnis bzw. ein Verbot
***Can** I use your internet to write emails to my parents?*	• eine Bitte
*This **can't** be true!*	• eine Möglichkeit oder eine Unmöglichkeit
*I **can** write again next week.*	• Zukünftiges (mit einer Zeitangabe der Zukunft)
	Could kann Folgendes ausdrücken:
*It was a pity that **I couldn't come** last year.*	• Vergangenheit *(konnte)*
***Could** we **go** to the beach?*	• Möglichkeit und Höflichkeit *(könnte)*.
*Julia and Stefan **will be able to** make themselves understood.*	*Can/could* als unvollständiges Hilfsverb kann nur im ***simple present*** und im ***simple past*** verwendet werden.
*They **will be allowed to use** the internet every day.*	Für alle anderen Zeiten braucht man die **Ersatzform *to be able to***, wenn eine Fähigkeit bezeichnet wird, oder die **Ersatzform *to be allowed to***, wenn man von einer Erlaubnis oder von einem Verbot spricht.

Merke

Neben den Hilfsverben, die dir helfen, die Zeiten zu bilden, gibt es die sogenannten modalen Hilfsverben, wie z. B. *can, may, must*. Sie drücken aus, ob Sprecher denken, dass das Subjekt eines Satzes etwas kann, darf, muss, also wie sie die Handlung, über die sie sprechen, persönlich einschätzen.
Modale Hilfsverben haben folgende Eigenschaften:

- Sie können nur im *simple present* und z. T. im *simple past* verwendet werden. Deshalb werden sie auch manchmal unvollständige Hilfsverben genannt.
- Bei der 3. Person Singular wird kein *-s* angehängt.
- Sie können – außer bei Frageanhängseln und Kurzantworten – nie allein stehen, sondern sie brauchen immer ein Vollverb (ohne *to*).
- Bei Fragen und Verneinungen braucht man keine Umschreibung mit *to do*, denn sie sind ja Hilfsverben, die helfen, Fragen und Verneinungen zu bilden.

Übung 1 **Julia telefoniert mit Katie. Vervollständige die Fragen, die sie sich stellen.**

Julia: .... Stefan and I stay with you in Canterbury?

Katie: Yes, you can.

Julia: .... the twins look after Stefan?

Katie: Yes, they can. But .... he look after himself?

Julia: Oh yes, he can. I meant: .... the twins show Stefan the sights and talk to him in English?

Katie: Of course they could. Will he .... speak a lot of English?

Julia: No, he won't. He could only speak very little English when we went to Malta last year.

Katie: But Stefan will .... make himself understood, won't he?

Julia: Oh yes, he will, but it won't be easy for him. By the way, will we .... use your computer to send emails?

Katie: Yes, you will if there are not too many.

Übung 2 **Übersetze die unterstrichenen modalen Hilfsverben. Achte auf die Zeiten.**

Stefan ist nicht glücklich darüber, dass er mit nach Großbritannien fahren soll. Seine Eltern versuchen, ihn zu überzeugen.

„Du bist nicht sehr gut in Englisch", sagt sein Vater. Du <u>hast noch nie</u> gute Noten erzielen <u>können</u> (...). Und erinnerst du dich, wie du auf Malta nur wenig auf Englisch sagen <u>konntest</u> (............................)?" „Das lag daran, dass ihr so gut Englisch sprechen <u>könnt</u> (..................................)," erwidert Stefan. „Ich hatte keine Möglichkeit." „Na ja, jetzt <u>könnte</u> (.............................) diese Reise dir eine gute Gelegenheit bieten", antwortet Julia. „Mandy und Mark, die in deinem Alter sind, <u>werden</u> dir alles zeigen <u>können</u> (...), und du <u>kannst</u> (.......................) nur Englisch mit ihnen sprechen, weil sie kein Deutsch <u>können</u> (..........................)." Stefan scheint sich mit der Idee anzufreunden. „Aber <u>werden</u> Mark und ich ohne Mandy Sport treiben <u>können</u> (.......................................)? Ich <u>könnte</u> es <u>nicht</u> (..............................) aushalten, mit einem Mädchen Fußball spielen zu müssen." „Wenn das dein einziges Problem ist", sagt sein Vater, „<u>können</u> (.............................) wir den Aufenthalt in England jetzt fest einplanen."

Lösungen Seite 101/102

2.2 Modale Hilfsverben *may/might/must/to be allowed to*

Alles klar?! ***May/might/must/be allowed to***

***May** I **ask** you a question?* *Yes, you **may**.* *Stefan's English **may improve** after his stay in England.*	***May** kann Folgendes ausdrücken:* • höfliche Bitte um Erlaubnis • Erlaubnis • Möglichkeiten, Vermutungen, Ungewissheiten
*Even Stefan **might like** it in Britain.* *I asked Mum if I **might go** to the cinema tonight.*	***Might** ist die höflichere Form.* • Mit *might* drückt man v.a. Möglichkeiten, Vermutungen, Ungewissheiten aus. • *Might* kann man auch Erlaubnis ausdrücken. Gewöhnlich steht es dann in der indirekten Rede.
*You **may not/must not** eat while you are watching TV.*	Mit *may not* und *must not* wird ein Verbot ausgedrückt. Dabei ist *may not* die höflichere Form.
*Julia and Stefan **will be allowed to use** the internet every day.*	*May* ist ein unvollständiges Hilfsverb, und es kann nur im ***simple present*** verwendet werden. Für alle anderen Zeiten und ein nicht so strenges Verbot verwendet man die **Ersatzform *to be allowed to*.**

Übung 1 **Stefan bereitet sich auf seinen Besuch bei den Johnsons vor. Kannst du ihm helfen, seine Fragen zu formulieren?**

Beispiel: What do I say if I am thirsty? May I have something to drink?

1. What do I say if I want to have an egg for breakfast?

....?

2. What do I say if I want to watch a football match on TV?

....?

3. What do I say if I want to phone my parents?

....?

4. What do I say if I want to borrow Mark's bike?

....?

5. What do I say if I want to use the Johnsons' internet?

....?

Lösungen Seite 102

Übung 2 **Stefan beschreibt seinen letzten Campingaufenthalt in einer E-Mail an Mark. Er möchte ihm erklären, welche Regeln sie beachten mussten.**

Beispiel: Length of stay one week only; no pets. We were allowed to stay one week only. We were not allowed to take any pets.

Do not pitch (= aufstellen) tents near the river.

....

No ball games close to the tents.

....

Do not use water from the river for cooking.

....

Take fresh water only from the well (= Brunnen).

....

Food may be cooked only outside the tents.

....

No loud music after 10 pm.

....

Lösungen Seite 102

2.3 Modale Hilfsverben *must/needn't/to have (got) to*

Alles klar?! ***Must/needn't/to have (got) to***

You ***must pack*** *your bag now.* *You* ***must be*** *tired. It was a long journey.*	***Must*** **kann Folgendes ausdrücken:** • eine Verpflichtung, einen Zwang, eine Notwendigkeit, eine Aufforderung • eine Wahrscheinlichkeit oder eine Gewissheit
You ***needn't bring*** *a lot of books. You can borrow mine.*	Die Verneinung von *must* lautet *needn't (= nicht brauchen).*
They ***will have to write*** *an email to their parents every day.* ***Did*** *they* ***have to write*** *an email to their parents?*	*Must* ist ein unvollständiges Hilfsverb, es kann nur im ***simple present*** verwendet werden. Für alle anderen Zeiten braucht man die **Ersatzform** ***to have (got) to***. Da *have* in diesem Fall ein Vollverb ist, ist bei Frage und Verneinung die Umschreibung mit *to do* notwendig.

Merke

Must und *to have to* kann man zwar beide mit *müssen* übersetzen, dennoch gibt es einen Bedeutungsunterschied.

- *Must* drückt ein persönliches Bedürfnis aus: *I must go to bed now. I'm so tired.*
- *To have to* wird verwendet, wenn man von einem äußeren Zwang spricht: *It's time for lunch. I have to finish now.*

Übung 1 **Stefans Vater spricht mit ihm über seinen bevorstehenden Besuch in England. Übersetze die unterstrichenen modalen Hilfsverben ins Englische.**

1. Du musst versuchen, immer freundlich zu sein.

....

2. Du brauchst uns nicht jeden Tag anzurufen, aber du musst uns eine E-Mail schreiben.

....

3. Du musst dich bedanken, wenn die Johnsons mit dir einen Ausflug machen.

....

4. Du brauchst nicht die ganze Zeit zu reden, aber du musst auf Fragen antworten.

....

Übung 2 **Setze *must/have to* ein.**

1. I .... go home now. I am so tired.
2. Mark's team has a football match on Saturday morning. He .... get up at 7 am.
3. It is 7.45 am and Mark has overslept. Now he .... hurry to be in time for the match.
4. On the way he meets Ben, who is also late. "We .... run as fast as we can or we will miss the match," Ben says.
5. Katie wants to go riding with Anne this weekend, but she cannot go with her. Anne says, "I .... visit my grandparents in Dover, it is grandmother's birthday."
6. Stefan's teacher said to him, "You .... work much harder if you want to get better grades in English."

2.4 Modales Hilfsverb *shall/should*

Alles klar?! ***Shall/should***

Shall *I* ***get*** *you something from Germany?* ***Shall*** *Stefan* ***bring*** *his tennis racket?*	***Shall*** **kann Folgendes ausdrücken:** • einen Wunsch erfragen • einen Vorschlag machen
You ***should speak*** *English all the time.* *We* ***should speak*** *English all the time.*	***Should*** **kann Folgendes ausdrücken:** • einen Ratschlag erteilen • eine Verpflichtung ausdrücken

Übung 1 **Benutze *shall*, um die folgenden Vorschläge in Fragen umzuwandeln.**

1. When Julia and Stefan come, I can bake a cake. ....?
2. We can invite some friends. ....?
3. I can put a 'welcome' sign on the front door. ....?
4. We could have a party. ....?

Übung 2 **Erteile Ratschläge.**

1. Stefan doesn't work very hard in his English lessons. He .... work harder.
2. Julia likes to tell Stefan what to do. She .... be so bossy.
3. Mark's room is very untidy. He .... put his things in the right place.
4. Mrs Grüner is worried about Stefan's visit to Britain. She .... worry about it; everything will be fine.
5. It's better to tell the truth. You .... always tell the truth.
6. Mandy is playing the recorder in the school concert, but she hasn't yet practised much. She .... practise more often.

Lösungen Seite 103

Übung 3 ★ **Setze *should* oder *shouldn't* mit dem passenden Verb ein, um Ratschläge oder Verpflichtungen auszudrücken.**

1. The twins watch too much television. They .... so much television.
2. My football boots are dirty. I .... them (to clean).
3. Mrs Johnson has put on weight. She .... (to do more sport).
4. Mrs Johnson: I am overweight. I .... to work by car (to go), I .... (to walk).
5. Mandy to Mark: We have been late for school every day this week. We .... earlier (to leave home).
6. Mr Johnson's car uses too much petrol. He .... a more economical one (to buy).
7. Katie looks ill this morning. She .... to school (to go).
8. It's very cold today. You .... a scarf for cycling (to wear).

Lösungen Seite 103

Abschlusstest (30 Minuten)

Aufgabe 1 **Setze die passenden modalen Hilfsverben ein: may/may not; might/might not; mustn't. Manchmal gibt es zwei Möglichkeiten.**

Katie is talking to the twins about Stefan's visit.

1. Stefan .... find it difficult to speak English.
2. He .... always understand what you say.
3. You .... speak too quickly.
4. If he makes a mistake, you .... laugh.
5. Mum .... give him some extra lessons in English.
6. And remember; Mandy, he .... want to play football with you.

Punkte: ☐ von 6

Aufgabe 2 **Stelle die Fragen und gib auch die Kurzantworten an, um eine Verpflichtung (bzw. das Gegenteil) auszudrücken. Achte auf die Zeiten.**

1. "............/Stefan/take/his German-English dictionary to England?"

   ....

   "No, he ...., Katie has one he can use."
2. "............/pupils/learn/all the English irregular verbs?"

   ....

   "No, they ...., but their English would certainly improve if they did."
3. "............/we/really go to bed now?" the twins ask their mother."

   ....

   "Yes, you ...., you both look very tired."
4. "............ Anne/visit/her grandparents recently?"

   ....

   "Yes, she .... It was her grandmother's birthday."

Lösungen Seite 103/104

5. " .... Katie/brush/her horse every time she has ridden him?"

....

"No, she .... She does it because she likes it."

6. " .... /you/make/such a mess in your bedroom?" Mrs Johnson asks Mark.

....

"No, I ...., but I like it that way."

Punkte: ☐ von 18

Aufgabe 3 **Setze die passenden modalen Hilfsverben ein, um eine Notwendigkeit, eine Verpflichtung, eine Vermutung (bzw. das Gegenteil) auszudrücken.**

Julia is phoning Katie.

Julia: I .... go to Portobello Road when we visit London.

Katie: Why do you want to go there?

Julia: I saw the film 'Notting Hill' recently and many of the scenes show the market in Portobello Road. It .... be very exciting to actually be there.

Katie: But we really .... bother to go; nobody ever finds anything worth buying. Grandma Booth says that you .... be very careful that you don't buy something worth nothing at all.

Julia: But I .... buy anything. I just want to enjoy the atmosphere.

Katie: Well, alright, if you really want to.

Julia: There is one thing I .... buy though. I just .... have the video of the film in English

Katie: You .... buy it; we have a copy at home that you can borrow.

Punkte: ☐ von 8

Lösungen Seite 104

Aufgabe 4 **Formuliere passende Vorschläge.**

1. You must be thirsty. .... /I/you/something to drink/get?

....

2. It is very hot in here. .... /open/the window/I?

....

3. Are you hungry? .... /get supper ready/we?

....

4. You both look very tired. .... /I/you/your rooms/show?

....

5. It's a lovely evening. .... /play/we/a game of tennis?

....

6. The sea looks beautiful. .... /go for a swim/we?

....

Punkte: ☐ von 6

Aufgabe 5 **Setze *shall/should/shouldn't* ein.**

1. It's a fine day. .... we have a picnic?
2. Mr Johnson's bike is covered in mud. He .... clean it.
3. We could sing some songs at the party. .... I bring my guitar?
4. Ben .... be in goal again; he let in five goals in the last match.
5. Julia loves horses; Katie .... let her brush Little Richard.
6. Stefan, you look bored. .... we play a game of chess?

Punkte: ☐ von 6

Punkte: ☐ von 44

34–44: Bravo! Du weißt schon gut Bescheid.
23–33: Teilweise bist du sicher, teilweise noch nicht. Bearbeite noch einmal die Übungen, in denen du beim ersten Mal viele Fehler hattest.
0–22: Leider ist dir noch zu vieles unklar. Arbeite das Kapitel noch einmal durch.

Lösungen Seite 104

3

Pronomen

Julia and Stefan are on their way to England and travel from Osnabrück to Calais on the French coast by train. In Calais they take the ferry across the English Channel to Dover. The Johnsons will be waiting in Dover to meet them from the ferry and take them back to Canterbury. Julia cannot remember much about her trip two years ago and Stefan is still not really sure he wants to go to England at all, especially as the weather is bad during the crossing, the sea is rough and he gets seasick.

3.1 *Reflexive Pronouns*

Alles klar?! ***myself, yourself, …***

Ergänze die Lücken.

Julia and Stefan carried all their bags ***themselves****.*	Reflexivpronomen werden verwendet, wenn sich eine Handlung auf den Handelnden rückbezieht. *Julia and Stefan carried all their bags* ***themselves****.* Die Reflexivpronomen werden mit der Endung *-self* im Singular und *-selves* im Plural gebildet. *my* .... *our* .... *your* .... *your* .... him .... *them* .... *her* .... *it* .... Es gibt auch noch eine unpersönliche Form: *one* .... Die Betonung der Reflexivpronomen liegt auf der zweiten Silbe.
They introduced ***themselves*** *to the Johnsons.* *They can look after* ***themselves.***	Oft stehen die Reflexivpronomen wie im Deutschen. Es gibt aber auch eine Reihe deutscher reflexiver Verben, deren englische Entsprechungen nicht reflexiv sind. Beispiele: *to behave* = sich benehmen *to change* = sich umziehen; sich ändern *to concentrate* = sich konzentrieren *to happen* = sich ereignen *to hurry* = sich beeilen *to be interested in* = sich interessieren *to meet* = sich treffen *to remember* = sich erinnern *to sit down* = sich setzen

Lösungen Seite 105

Lerntipp
Es gibt einige feste Wendungen mit Reflexivpronomen, die besonders nützlich sind. Kennst du schon ihre deutsche Bedeutung? Vor allem die ersten beiden werden Julia und Stefan sicher bei ihrem Besuch bei den Johnsons hören.

Help yourself/yourselves. ....

Enjoy yourself/yourselves. ....

I did it all by myself. ....

Übung 1 **Ergänze das Reflexivpronomen.**

1. Stefan has been sick on the ferry, he is feeling very sorry for ....
2. When they arrive in Dover, Julia and Stefan carry their bags ....
3. When they meet the Johnsons, they introduce ....
4. Katie has looked after Stefan on the journey and is proud of ....
5. As he was getting off the ferry Stefan fell down and hurt ....
6. Katie is sure she will enjoy .... in England.
7. A cat can get down from a tree ....
8. „We were very proud of .... at the end of the journey," Katie wrote to her mother.

Übung 2 **Setze die Reflexivpronomen ein.**

Tea-time at the Johnsons. Mrs Johnson says:

Welcome to Canterbury, Julia and Stefan, we are very pleased to see you. We always have tea at this time, so please help .... Mark and Mandy helped me to make the sandwiches before we left for Dover and Mark was a little clumsy (= ungeschickt) and cut .... with a knife. The cake is a typically English fruit cake, I made it .... We often ask .... what sort of meals you have in Germany and hope you like the English food. We hope to visit Germany one day .... and then we will learn what it is like. Anyway, now you are here and we hope you will enjoy ....

Lösungen Seite 105

Übung 3 **Reflexiv oder nicht? Übersetze die Verben ins Englische.**

1. Julia und Stefan setzten sich an den Tisch. ....
2. Sie waren stolz auf sich, die Reise alleine gemacht zu haben. ....
   ....
3. Frau Johnson hat den Kuchen selbst gebacken. ....
4. Katie und die Zwillinge freuten sich über den Besuch. ....
5. Julia war sehr müde und musste sich auf das Gespräch sehr konzentrieren.
   ....
6. Morgen werden sie sich mit Freunden in der Stadt treffen. ....

Übung 4 ★ **Suche das passende Verb und vervollständige die Sätze. Sind die Verben reflexiv oder nicht?**

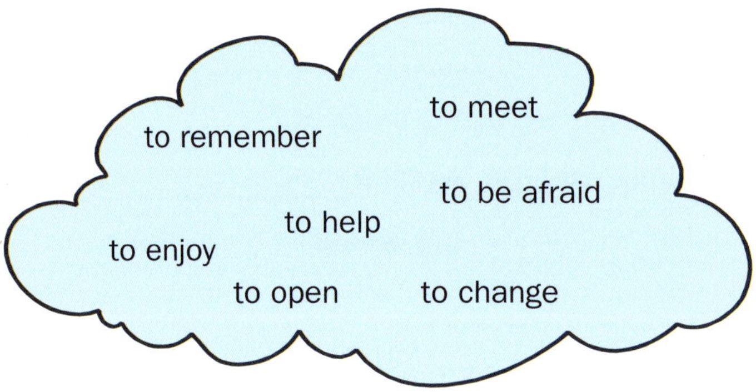

1. The door to Julia's room .... and Katie came in with a cup of tea.
2. She told Julia to .... so they could go and explore the town.
3. She said, they would .... her friend Mary in a café and ....
4. "Don't ...., she is very friendly," she said.
5. "I can .... the cathedral," said Julia, "I have seen it before."
6. When they get home they will .... to some tea and cake.

Lösungen Seite 105

3.2 *Reciprocal Pronouns*

Alles klar?! ***each other/one another***

They helped ***each other/one another*** *to carry their bag.*

Reziproke Pronomen beschreiben ein gegenseitiges, wechselbezügliches Verhältnis:

sie helfen sich (gegenseitig)

Im Deutschen wird in solchen Fällen ein **Reflexivpronomen** verwendet

Übung 1 **Vervollständige die Sätze. Verwende *each other/one another* oder das richtige Reflexivpronomen.**

1. Katie and Anne live near ....
2. When they go riding together they always enjoy ....
3. Stefan and Mark have not met before, they do not know ....
4. Anne, don't brush Little Richard, I'd like to do it ....
5. When it is the twins' birthday, they always give .... presents.
6. Julia and Katie are penfriends, they often write to ....

Übung 2 **Vervollständige die Sätze mit Satzteilen aus der Wolke.**

help yourselves
look after themselves
to help each other
talk to each other
look after each other
talk to themselves

1. Now that the Booths are older, they often ....
2. Mr and Mrs Booth were ill, so they had to ....
3. Mark and Ben can ...., they are good at judo.
4. Katie and Mary like riding together; it gives them time to ....
5. The twins do not need help from Katie, they can ....
6. Please, ..., I hope you enjoy the meal.

Lösungen Seite 106

3.3 Prop Word one/ones

Alles klar?! ***one/ones***

*I like all those seagulls. Look at the **cheeky one** over there. It is stealing the man's sandwich.*

Wenn ein zählbares Substantiv nicht wiederholt werden soll, wird ein **Stützwort** eingesetzt: ***one*** für Singular und ***ones*** für Plural.

Übrigens: Im Deutschen reicht es in solchen Fällen, wenn einfach das Adjektiv wiederholt wird:

*„Ich mag die Möwen. Schau dir die **freche** dort drüben an. Sie stiehlt dem Mann das Sandwich."*

Im Englischen kann das Adjektiv nicht alleine stehen. Es muss durch *one/ones* **gestützt** werden.

Übung 1 **Vervollständige die Sätze mit *one/ones*.**

1. "Katie, please lend me your pen to write my postcard." "Sorry Julia, I haven't got ...."
2. Which sunglasses shall we buy for Dad, the black .... or the brown ....?
3. The twins have a cat, it is a black ....
4. Let's buy these shoes, Katie, they look smarter than the blue ....
5. England has many cathedrals but Canterbury is a very famous ....
6. Which postcard shall I send Uncle Alan in Boston, this .... or that ....?

Übung 2 **Brauchst du hier das Stützwort? Setze ein, wo nötig.**

1. Katie, which .... would you like to ride: the black horse or the brown ....?
2. Would you like this card or that ....? Both ...., please.
3. Katie's horse is fast, but Anne's horse is the faster ....
4. Mark was the first .... of the twins to be born.
5. Mark's friend Ben has three sisters. Each .... is pretty.
6. Canterbury and Dover are both popular tourist resorts but Dover is the .... nearer the sea.

Lösungen Seite 106

Abschlusstest (25 Minuten)

Aufgabe 1 **Übersetze die folgenden Sätze ins Englische.**

1. Julia und Katie haben sich in der Stadt sehr amüsiert.

....

2. Setz dich und bediene dich!

....

3. Ich habe den Kuchen selbst gebacken.

....

4. Die Fähre wird pünktlich ankommen, wir machen uns keine Sorgen.

....

Punkte: ☐ von 4

Aufgabe 2 **Setze das richtige Pronomen ein: Manchmal wird keines gebraucht!**

1. Be careful of the candle, you might burn ....
2. Mary did not have riding lessons, she taught .... to ride.
3. Katie and Julia met .... in town to visit the cathedral.
4. They have been writing to .... for two years.
5. Katie fell off Little Richard and broke .... her arm.
6. She must concentrate .... better or she will fall off again.

Punkte: ☐ von 6

Aufgabe 3 **Wähle das richtige Pronomen und markiere es.**

1. In the summer holidays Katie and Mary don't see themselves/each other very often.
2. Mandy and I give us/ourselves/each other presents on our birthday.
3. My mother always bakes the cakes –/herself.
4. Mrs Johnson and her brother Alan were talking to each other/themselves on the phone.
5. Ben loves judo, he can't imagine –/himself doing any other sport.

Punkte: ☐ von 5

Lösungen Seite 106/107

Aufgabe 4 **Bilde Sätze und ergänze Reflexivpronomen, reziproke Pronomen oder Stützwort, falls notwendig.**

1. There/to be/in the garden/tall tree and/a short.

....

2. Mark and Mandy/to understand/always/without speaking.

....

3. They/to see/seldom/in the mirror.

....

4. There/to be/in the vase/pink flower and/a blue.

....

5. The Johnsons' cat/clean/every day.

....

6. Ben/to enjoy/usually/at judo club.

....

Punkte: ☐ von 6

Aufgabe 5 **Vervollständige Julias Fragen an Katie mit *one/ones* und einem Wortpaar.**

first/second | blue/red | small/big | French/German | old/new | leather/canvas

1. Which desk is yours – the .... or the ....
2. Which pen do you use – the .... or the ....
3. Which lesson do you prefer – the .... or the ....
4. Which book are you reading – the .... or the ....
5. Which lunch break shall we take – the .... or the ....
6. Which schoolbag is yours – the .... or the ....

Punkte: ☐ von 12

Punkte: ☐ von 33

27–33: Bravo! Du weißt schon gut Bescheid.
17–26: Teilweise bist du sicher, teilweise noch nicht. Bearbeite noch einmal die Übungen, in denen du beim ersten Mal viele Fehler hattest.
0–16: Leider ist dir noch zu vieles unklar. Arbeite das Kapitel noch einmal durch.

 Lösungen Seite 107

4

Passiv

Stefan and Julia have settled into life with the Johnsons although Stefan finds English food a little strange sometimes. On his first morning he was offered bacon and eggs for breakfast; this was quite a change from the muesli and toast he usually eats at home. Another surprise was his visit to the Cathedral. He had expected to find it boring, but when he heard about the murder of Thomas Beckett, he just couldn't wait to see exactly where the Archbishop had been killed.

4.1 Unterscheidung Aktiv/Passiv

Alles klar?! **Verwendung**

Normalerweise stehen Sätze im Aktiv: Ein Subjekt führt eine Tätigkeit (= Prädikat) aus, darauf folgt die Person oder Sache (= Objekt), der etwas „getan" wird.

Guides	*show*	*the Cathedral*	*to many people.*
subject (active)	**predicate**	**object**	

Wenn man besonders hervorheben will, was mit dem Objekt geschieht, oder wenn man nicht weiß, wer etwas getan hat, oder wenn es egal ist, wer etwas getan hat, dann kann man einen Satz im **Passiv** bilden.
Das Objekt des Aktivsatzes wird zum Subjekt des Passivsatzes.

The Cathedral	*is shown*	*to many people*	*(by guides).*
subject (passive)	**predicate**	**object**	

Lerntipp
Wenn du im Passivsatz noch sagen willst, wer die Handlung verursacht hat, kannst du den sogenannten ***by-agent*** verwenden, d. h., du stellst das **Subjekt** des Passivsatzes mit der Präposition *by* **ans Ende des Satzes**.

Übung 1 **Bilde Aktivsätze aus den folgenden Passivsätzen**

1. Julia and Stefan were met at Dover by the Johnsons.
2. They were given a warm welcome by the whole family.
3. Stefan and Julia were served a typical English breakfast by Mrs Johnson.
4. Julia was told about Canterbury's history by Katie.
5. In the evening a huge meal was cooked by Katie and Mrs Johnson.
6. Mark found a dead mouse, which had been caught by Maggie.
7. Thousands of postcards are bought by visitors every year.
8. Stefan will be shown round Canterbury by the twins.

Lösungen Seite 107

4.2 Das Passiv in verschiedenen Zeiten

Alles klar?! **So bildest du das Passiv**

The oldest part of the Cathedral ***was built*** *in the Middle Ages.*

Das Passiv wird gebildet:
- mit dem Hilfsverb *be*, das jeweils in der entsprechenden Personal- und Zeitform steht,
- mit dem *past participle* (Partizip Perfekt).

Du weißt jetzt schon so viel, dass du die einzelnen Zeitformen im Passiv selbstständig bilden kannst. Ergänze jeweils die hinterlegten Kästchen.

Simple present – passive: *to be* im *simple present (= am, is, are)* + *past participle* des Vollverbs

Guides	*tell*	*interesting facts*	*about the Cathedral.*
Interesting facts	....		*about the Cathedral.*

Simple past – passive: *to be* im *simple past (= was, were)* + *past participle* des Vollverbs

Murderers	*killed*	*Thomas Beckett*	*in the Cathedral.*
Thomas Beckett	....		*in the Cathedral.*

Present perfect – passive: *to be* im *present perfect (= have/has been)* + *past participle* des Vollverbs

More visitors than ever	*have visited*	*the Cathedral*	*this year.*
The Cathedral	....	*by more visitors than ever*	*this year.*

Future – passive: *to be* im *future (= will be)* + *past participle* des Vollverbs

Visitors	*will learn*	*a lot*	*in a guided tour.*
A lot	....		*in a guided tour.*

Und dann noch mit **modalem Hilfsverb:** modales Hilfsverb + *be* + *past participle* des Vollverbs

They	*can see*	*a lot of colourful windows*	*in the Cathedral.*
A lot of colourful windows	....		*in the Cathedral.*

Lösungen Seite 108

Übung 1 **Setze die folgenden Sätze ins Passiv ohne den *by-agent*. Achte auf die Zeiten.**

1. The Normans rebuilt the Cathedral in the 11th century.

2. Katie took Julia and Stefan to the Cathedral.

3. She told Stefan about the murder.

4. People have written many books about the murder.

5. You can take photographs of the beautiful windows.

6. Henry the Eighth closed the monastery (= Kloster) in 1540.

7. Every year musicians hold concerts in the Cathedral.

8. Mrs Johnson will wake the twins at 7 am.

9. Julia has warned Stefan about the traffic on the left.

10. Stefan cannot find the new word in the dictionary.

Lösungen Seite 109

Übung 2 **Bilde Passivsätze mit dem *by-agent*. Achte auf die Zeiten.**

1. Thousands of tourists/to visit/the Cathedral/every week.

....

2. The visitors/to take, always/a great number of photographs.

....

3. Soldiers/to smash (= zertrümmern)/many beautiful windows/in the 17th century.

....

4. Craftsmen/the windows/to repair.

....

5. Mr Johnson/to drive/Mark/to the football match/next Saturday.

....

6. Mrs Johnson/to make, just/a lot of cakes.

....

7. Katie/to ride/Little Richard/every week.

....

8. The choir/to sing/some very beautiful songs/at the concert yesterday.

....

Lösungen Seite 109

4.3 Besondere Formen

Alles klar?! ***Verbs with Prepositions***

Auch mit **Verben**, die eng mit einer **Präposition** verbunden sind, können Passivsätze gebildet werden.

Die Präposition gehört dabei so eng zum Verb, dass sie auch im Passivsatz direkt auf das Verb folgt:

Visitors	*will **find out***	*interesting facts*	*in a guided tour.*
Interesting facts	*will be **found out***		*in a guided tour.*

Weitere Verben mit Präpositionen:

to break into	einbrechen	*to think of*	denken an
to laugh at	lachen über	*to talk about*	reden über
to look after	sich kümmern um	*to speak to*	sprechen mit
to look at	anschauen	*to read to*	vorlesen

Übung 1 **Verwandle die Aktivsätze ins Passiv mit *by-agent*.**

1. A burglar (= Einbrecher) broke into a number of houses.

....

2. Mrs Johnson often reads to Stefan in English.

....

3. Mr and Mrs Johnson talked about Stefan's language problems.

....

4. Stefan's parents looked at the photos of Canterbury Cathedral.

....

5. The audience laughed at the clown's tricks.

....

6. Anne will look after Maggie when the Johnsons are away.

....

Lösungen Seite 109

Übung 2 ★ **Bilde Passivsätze.**

1. At the meeting yesterday/to think of/a lot of new ideas.

....

2. Mark's school bag/all the family/to look for/every morning.

....

3. The teacher/to speak to/last week/Mark's parents.

....

4. To feed and play with/the twins/Maggie/twice today.

....

5. Mark and Mandy's old toys/Mrs Johnson/to throw away, must.

....

6. The entrance fees/to pay for (Futur)/Mr Johnson.

....

Alles klar?! ***Passive – Verbs with two Objects***

Es gibt Verben, die zwei Objekte haben:

- ein direktes oder Akkusativobjekt (wen oder was?),
- ein indirektes oder Dativobjekt (wem?).

Mit Verben dieser Art können zwei Formen des Passivs gebildet werden:

They	*offered*	***the visitors***	***a guided tour.***
subject	predicate	indirect object (wem?)	direct object *(wen oder was?)*

1. Das *indirekte Objekt* wird zum Subjekt des Passivsatzes

The visitors	*were offered*	*a guided tour.*
subject	predicate	direct object *(wen oder was?)*

Diese Form des Passivs wird ***persönliches Passiv*** genannt. Es wird oft verwendet, wenn im Deutschen *man* oder *jemand* gesagt würde: *Jemand hat den Besuchern eine Führung angeboten.*

Lösungen Seite 109

2. Das *direkte Objekt* wird zum Subjekt des Passivsatzes

A guided tour	*was offered*	***(to)** the visitors.*
subject	predicate	indirect object *(wem?)*

Diese Konstruktion wird nur verwendet, wenn das *direkte Objekt* des Aktivsatzes besonders hervorgehoben werden soll. Das *indirekte Objekt* kann dann mit oder ohne *to* stehen.

Weitere Verben mit zwei Objekten:

to ask	fragen	*to sell*	verkaufen
to give	geben	*to send*	schicken
to lend	leihen	*to show*	zeigen
to pay	zahlen	*to teach*	lehren
to promise	versprechen	*to tell*	erzählen

Lerntipp

Wenn das indirekte Objekt ein Pronomen ist, steht es in der Objektform. Wenn es an Subjektposition tritt, muss es in die Subjektform umgewandelt werden.

Für dich ist es sicher überhaupt kein Problem, die Subjektform der Pronomen hier einzusetzen.

They offered me a guided tour.	.... was offered a guided tour.
They offered you a guided tour.	.... were offered a guided tour.
They offered him a guided tour.	.... was offered a guided tour.
They offered her a guided tour.	.... was offered a guided tour.
They offered us a guided tour.	.... were offered a guided tour.
They offered you a guided tour.	.... were offered a guided tour.
They offered them a guided tour.	.... were offered a guided tour.

Lösungen Seite 110

Übung 3 **Forme die Aktivsätze in Passivsätze um. Verwende das *persönliche Passiv* ohne *by-agent*.**

1. The Cathedral offers all visitors a warm welcome.

....

2. Guides show visitors the Cathedral.

....

3. King Ethelbert gave the first Archbishop a church in Canterbury.

....

4. Katie told Stefan the story of Thomas Beckett's murder.

....

5. Stefan sent Jan some pictures of the Cathedral.

....

6. Mrs Johnson promised Stefan a visit to the Edinburgh Tattoo.

....

Übung 4 **Übersetze die folgenden Sätze ins Englische. Verwende das *persönliche Passiv.***

1. Man muss die alten Häuser abreißen.

....

2. Man kann den Kathedralenführer (= the Cathedral guide book) im Souvenirladen kaufen.

....

3. Man zeigte den Touristen die Stadt.

....

4. Man hat der Schule zehn neue Computer versprochen.

....

5. Man erzählte den Besuchern einige interessante Tatsachen.

....

6. Man verkauft Stadtpläne von Canterbury in jedem großen Laden.

....

Lösungen Seite 110

Übung 5 ★ **Verwandle die folgenden Sätze in die *jeweils andere Passivform* für Verben mit zwei Objekten.**

1. An umbrella was lent to Julia.

....

2. A new bicycle has been promised to Mark.

....

3. A guidebook was sold to Julia.

....

4. The beautiful coastline was shown to Julia and Stefan.

....

5. A new song was taught to the choir.

....

6. Five pounds were paid to Mark to cut the grass.

....

Übung 6 ★ **Bilde persönliche Passivsätze ohne *by-agent*. Beginne den Satz mit dem passenden Pronomen.**

Beispiel: Mr Walters taught the twins the recorder. They were taught the recorder.

1. Stefan asked Katie a question.

....

2. Mrs Johnson lent Stefan a dictionary.

....

3. Herr Grüner promised Stefan a new computer.

....

4. Julia sent her parents an email.

....

5. Will the guide tell us some interesting stories?

....

6. He will give you a fascinating tour of the town.

....

Lösungen Seite 110

Alles klar?! ***The Impersonal Passive***

It is reported that Thomas Beckett was killed in the Cathedral.

Mit dem Subjekt *it* und Verben des Sagens und Denkens wird das sogenannte ***unpersönliche Passiv*** gebildet, das oft mit dem deutschen *man* übersetzt wird:

Man berichtet/es wird berichtet, dass ...

Weitere Beispiele:

it is believed	man glaubt
it is feared	man befürchtet/es wird befürchtet
it is known	man weiß
it is said	man berichtet
it is thought	man glaubt/man meint
it is understood	man nimmt an/es wird angenommen

Übung 7 ★ **Übersetze die unterstrichenen Satzteile ins Englische, und verwende das *unpersönliche Passiv*.**

The murder of Thomas Beckett

Man weiß that Thomas Beckett was killed in the Cathedral. Es wird berichtet that four knights were the murderers. Es wird behauptet that the king and Thomas Beckett were once good friends. Man glaubt that Thomas Beckett became more loyal to the Pope than to the king once he was made Archbishop of Canterbury. Man meint that the king was angry with Thomas Beckett for many different reasons. Es wird angenommen that the four knights really thought that the king wanted Thomas Beckett to die. Man berichtet that the king later went on a pilgrimage (= Wallfahrt) to Canterbury, barefoot and in sackcloth, to show his sorrow (= Reue).

 Lösungen Seite 111

Abschlusstest (20 Minuten)

Aufgabe 1 **Vervollständige die Sätze mit der Passivform.**

1. Tennis .... (to play, sometimes) at the twin's school.
2. More vegetables than fruit .... (to grow) in the Johnsons' garden.
3. What kind of cake .... (to sell) at the shop?
4. Do you know where the tennis balls .... (to keep)?
5. How often .... (to collect, rubbish) in Canterbury?
6. Why .... (to worry, Frau Grüner) about Stefan's visit to England?

Punkte: ☐ von 6

Aufgabe 2 **Setze die Sätze ins Passiv mit *by-agent*.**

1. The visitors have bought thousands of postcards.

   ....

2. Volunteers serve tea and cakes in the Cathedral restaurant.

   ....

3. The Johnsons took Julia and Stefan to the funfair.

   ....

4. Guides will show the visitors where Thomas Beckett died.

   ....

5. Mr Johnson cuts the grass every week.

   ....

6. Katie has broken Mrs Johnson's favourite necklace.

   ....

Punkte: ☐ von 6

Lösungen Seite 111

Aufgabe 3 **Bilde Passivsätze aus den Satzteilen.**

All mobile phones	to clear away	after the party
Library books	to fix up (= arrangieren)	soon
Mark's room	to cut down	on Saturdays
Most of the football matches	to switch off, must	last week
The old oak tree	to tidy up, must	immediately
The plates and dishes	to give back, cannot	for the next season

Punkte: ☐ von 6

Aufgabe 4 **Übersetze die folgenden Sätze ins Englische.**

1. Man weiß, dass Elefanten sehr alt werden können.
2. Little Richard wird jeden Tag gebürstet.
3. Ich hoffe, dass dein Zimmer bald aufgeräumt wird.
4. Das Geschäft ist geschlossen worden.
5. Es wird angenommen, dass die Lehrer nicht streiken.
6. Den Besuchern wurde ein Film gezeigt.
7. In der neuen Schule werden drei Sprachen unterrichtet.
8. Auf der Feier wurden viele Witze erzählt.
9. Mir wurden zehn Euro geliehen./Man hat mir zehn Euro geliehen.
10. Das seltsame Insekt wurde lange betrachtet.

Punkte: ☐ von 10

Punkte: ☐ von 28

23–28: Bravo! Du weißt schon gut Bescheid.
15–22: Teilweise bist du sicher, teilweise noch nicht. Bearbeite noch einmal die Übungen, in denen du beim ersten Mal viele Fehler hattest.
0–14: Leider ist dir noch zu vieles unklar. Arbeite das Kapitel noch einmal durch.

Lösungen Seite 111

5 Indirekte Rede

Julia and Stefan are excited; the Johnsons are planning a trip to London to show them such famous sights as Buckingham Palace, the Tower of London and Westminster Abbey. Stefan is particularly interested in the London Eye, a large Ferris wheel, the wax figures at Madame Tussaud's and the Millennium Bridge while Julia hopes to find time to go shopping in Oxford Street with Katie and perhaps see a musical in the West End.

5.1 *Direct Speech/Reported Speech*

Alles klar?! **Umwandlung direkte Rede – indirekte Rede**

Julia says, "I want to walk across the Millennium Bridge."	Wenn man etwas wiederholen will, was eine andere Person gesagt hat, kann man das wörtlich tun oder …
Julia says (that) she wants to walk across the Millennium Bridge.	… man verwendet **indirekte Rede/*reported speech***.
	Eingeleitet wird die indirekte Rede durch ein Verb des Sagens *(reporting verb)*, wie *to say, to answer, to think*. Hier schließt sich ein Nebensatz mit *that* an, vor dem **kein** Komma steht. Das *that* kann auch weggelassen werden. *Julia says (that) she wants to walk across the Millennium Bridge.* • Hauptsatz mit Verb des Sagens • Nebensatz durch *that* eingeleitet
Stefan says (that) he wants to go to Madame Tussaud's.	Wenn sofort wiedergegeben wird, was jemand gesagt hat, steht das einleitende Verb im ***simple present***.
Stefan said (that) he wanted to go to Madame Tussaud's.	Wenn erst später wiedergegeben wird, was jemand gesagt hat, steht das einleitende Verb in einer Zeitform der Vergangenheit. Die Zeitform des Verbs im Nebensatz wird gegenüber der wörtlichen Rede um eine Stufe zurückversetzt (siehe Seite 57).

Übung 1 **In dieser Buchstabenschlange haben sich mehrere Verben des Sagens versteckt. Suche sie heraus.**

qutewndtoanswerforetosayvkfedtoreportfkwüdtotellmreftoremark-burlftoreplymwptfsdvtoagreekbmeoftoexplainlhnrtothinknmeigej

Lösungen Seite 112

Merke

Wenn du eine Aussage einer anderen Person in die indirekte Rede setzt, passiert etwas ganz automatisch: Du passt die Pronomen deinem Standpunkt an.

	direkte Rede	**indirekte Rede**
Personalpronomen	*I, you* *we, you*	*he/she* *they*
Possessivpronomen	*my, your* *our, your*	*his/her* *their*
Objektpronomen	*me, you* *us, you*	*him/her* *them*
Demonstrativpronomen (-artikel)	*this* *these*	*that* *those*

Übung 2 **Was sagen die Leute?**

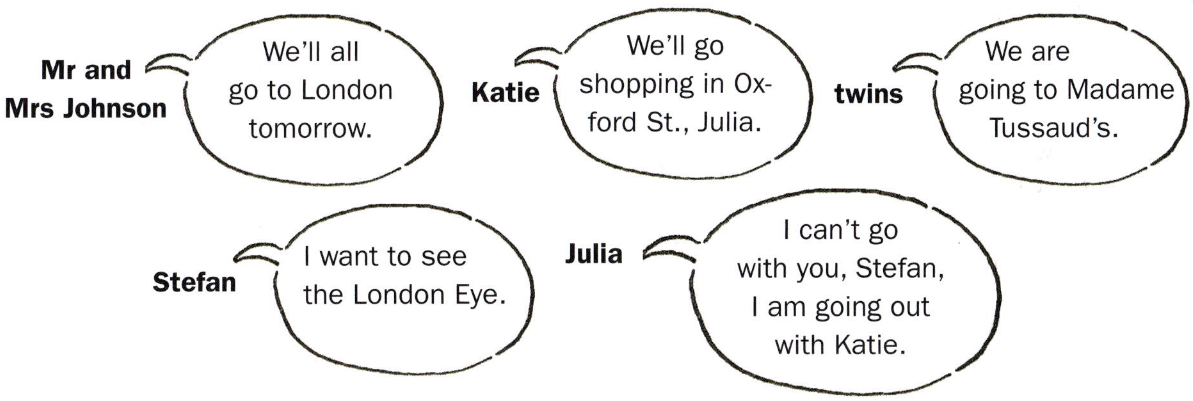

1. Mr and Mrs Johnson explain that ....
2. Katie tells Julia that ....
3. The twins explain that ....
4. Stefan says that ....
5. Julia informs Stefan that .... because

   she ....

Lösungen Seite 112

Übung 3 **Ergänze die Lücken.**

Mrs Johnson has been at home all day and has listed the phone calls she has received.

Mother-no tickets for MT
Train 8 am
Anne for Katie re LR
Ben judo class
Dad, train late

Mrs Johnson tells the family:

1. "Mandy, Grandma Booth called, ... can't get tickets for .... for Madame Tussaud's."
2. "Katie, Anne called. Can you ring .... back, ... wants to tell .... something about Little Richard."
3. "I called the station. They said if .... want to be in London before 10 .... must catch the train at 8 am."
4. "Mark, Ben called. .... can't go with .... to judo class this evening."
5. "Dad called. .... missed his train, ... won't be home in time to have supper with .... "

Übung 4 **Wandle die Sätze in die direkte Rede um.**

1. Katie tells her mother that she and Julia are going to go shopping in London.
   Katie to her mother: ....
2. Julia says she has left her map of London at home.
   Julia: ....
3. Mr Johnson doesn't think that the girls should go shopping alone.
   Mr Johnson to the girls: ....
4. Mrs Johnson told Mark that he and Mandy can't go to Madame Tussaud's on their own.
   Mrs Johnson: ....

Lösungen Seite 112

5.2 *Backshift of Tenses*

Alles klar?! **Das musst du bei der *indirekten Rede* beachten**

Wenn das die **indirekte Rede** einleitende Verb in einer Zeitform der Vergangenheit steht, wird die Zeitform des Verbs im Nebensatz gegenüber der wörtlichen Rede um **eine Stufe zurückversetzt (backshift)**.

Simple present → simple past

Julia said,	*"I*	***like***	*the Millennium Bridge very much."*
Julia said (that)	*she*	***liked***	*the Millennium Bridge very much.*

Present progressive → past progressive

Stefan said,	*"We*	***are having***	*a great time at Madame Tussaud's."*
Stefan said (that)	*they*	***were having***	*a great time at Madame Tussaud's.*

Present perfect → past perfect

Stefan said,	*"I*	***have** never **seen** such a big Ferris wheel as the London Eye."*
Stefan said,	*he*	***had** never **seen** such a big Ferris wheel as the London Eye.*

Going-to* future → *was/were going to

Mrs Johnson said,	*"Oh no, it'**s going***		*to rain."*
Mrs Johnson said (that)	*it*	***was going***	*to rain.*

***Will-future* → *would* + infinitive**

Stefan said,	*"I*	***will** certainly **come***	*back to London."*
Stefan said (that)	*he*	***would** certainly **come***	*back to London.*

Achtung

Wenn man Aussagen in die indirekte Rede setzt, die nach wie vor gültig sind, dann ist manchmal der *backshift* des Verbtempus nicht nötig.
Julia said, "I will always like London." → *Julia said she will always like London.*

Übung 1 **Wandle die Sätze in die indirekte Rede um.**

Julia und Stefan telefonieren mit ihren Eltern.
Julia said that ...

1. Julia: I like London very much, there is so much to see.
2. Stefan: Yes, we are having a wonderful time.
3. Julia: I love shopping in Oxford St., I have never seen so many interesting shops and people from all over the world.
4. Stefan: I am sure Julia has spent all her holiday money.
5. Julia: No, I haven't! We are going to the London Eye tomorrow and I need some money for postcards.
6. Stefan: I have posted all my cards to my friends and I have written them all in English.
7. Julia: We really must go and buy an umbrella, it's going to rain.
8. Stefan: We will phone again soon; we're going to have so much to tell you when we get home, it will take us hours!

Lösungen Seite 112

5.3 *Reported Speech with Auxiliary Verbs*

Alles klar?! ***Reported Speech with Auxiliary Verbs***

can → could/was able to/was allowed to

Mrs Johnson said,	*"We*	***can't go***	*to London Zoo."*
Mrs Johnson said (that)	*they*	***couldn't go/weren't able to go***	*to London Zoo.*

may → might

Mrs Johnson said,	*"We*	***may do***	*a boat trip."*
Mrs Johnson said (that)	*they*	***might do***	*a boat trip.*

must → must/had to

Mrs Johnson said,	*"We*	***must take/have to take***	*the train at five."*
Mrs Johnson said (that)	*they*	***must take/had to take***	*the train at five.*

Übung 1 **Wandle die Sätze in die *direkte* Rede um.**

What did Mrs Johnson say?

1. Mrs Johnson said that they had to take the train at eight o'clock.

....

2. Mrs Johnson said they might take a boat on the Thames to Hampton Court.

....

3. Mrs Johnson said they couldn't go to Madame Tussaud's but they were able to go to the London Eye.

....

4. Mrs Johnson said they had to take an umbrella in case it rained.

....

Lösungen Seite 113

5.4 *Questions*

Alles klar?! **Fragen mit und ohne Fragewort**

Fragen ohne Fragewort

Backshift wie im Aussagesatz – Einfügung vom *if/whether* (= ob) – Wortstellung wie im Aussagesatz:

Stefan asked,		*"Can we go to London again?"*
Stefan asked	*if/whether*	*they could go to London again.*

Fragen mit Fragewort

Backshift wie im Aussagesatz – Fragewort bleibt erhalten – Wortstellung wie im Aussagesatz:

Stefan asked,	*"**When** can we go to London again?"*
Stefan asked	***when** they could go to London again.*

Übung 1 **Gib die Fragen in der indirekten Rede wieder.**

What did they ask?

1. Julia asked, "Where can we go shopping?"

....

2. Stefan asked, "When can we go to the London Eye?"

....

3. Julia asked, "Can we see a musical in the West End?"

....

4. The Johnsons asked, "Do you want to see the Millennium Bridge?"

....

Lösungen Seite 113

5.5 *Commands and Requests*

Alles klar?! ***Commands and Requests***

Ein Befehl oder eine Aufforderung wird in der **indirekten Rede** meist mit den Verben *to tell* oder *to ask* wiedergegeben:

Mrs Johnson shouted, "Hurry up."
Mrs Johnson told them to hurry up.

Mrs Johnson asked, "Can you please hurry up?"
Mrs Johnson asked them to hurry up.

- *to tell someone to do something* – jemandem sagen, dass er/sie etwas tun soll
- *to ask someone to do something* – jemanden bitten/auffordern, etwas zu tun

Übung 1 **Gib die Aufforderung in der direkten Rede wieder.**

What did they say?

1. Katie asked the twins to meet her at 6 o'clock.

....

2. Mark asked his father to take them to the London Eye.

....

3. Julia asked Katie to tell her the history of Hampton Court.

....

4. Mrs Johnson told them to be quiet.

....

Lösungen Seite 113

5.6 *Adverbials of Place and Time*

Alles klar?! ***Adverbials of Place and Time***

Ähnlich wie die Pronomina müssen die **Orts- und Zeitangaben** auch an den Standpunkt des Sprechers angepasst werden.

Mrs Johnson said, "We can't go to London Zoo today."
Mrs Johnson said (that) they couldn't go to London Zoo that day.

Weitere Beispiele für Orts- und Zeitangaben, die verändert werden:

yesterday	*the day before, the previous day*
tomorrow	*the next day, the following day*
now	*then, at that time*
two weeks ago	*two weeks before*
next week	*the following week*
here	*there, in that place (genaue Ortsangabe)*

Übung 1 **Wie lauten die Orts- und Zeitangaben bei der direkten Rede?**

1. The twins said they couldn't go to the Millennium Bridge that day. ....
2. They told Julia they had been there the day before. ....
3. Katie said she would go shopping with Julia in Oxford St. the next day. ....
4. She said they would see many tourists there. ....
5. Julia said she and Stefan had arrived in Canterbury two weeks before. ....
6. Mr Johnson said they would return to Canterbury the following week. ....

Lösungen Seite 113

Abschlusstest (30 Minuten)

Aufgabe 1 **Setze die folgenden Sätze in die indirekte Rede.**

1. Julia: Stefan and I have been in England for two weeks.

   Julia said that Stefan and ....

2. Stefan: I am not very good at English yet.

   Stefan said that he ....

3. Mandy: I don't really like shopping in big cities.

   Mandy has just told me ....

4. Mark: Can I go to London Zoo?

   Mark has just asked ....

5. Stefan: When can we go to the Hard Rock Café?

   Stefan asked ....

6. Katie: I hope we will be able to come to London again.

   Katie said ....

7. Mrs Johnson: Hurry up, please, we'll miss the train.

   Mrs Johnson told ....

Punkte: ☐ von 7

Aufgabe 2 **Verwandle die Sätze in die direkte Rede zurück.**

1. Stefan said he hoped he would be able to see the London Eye.

   Stefan: ....

2. Mark said he did not know where the Millennium Bridge was.

   Mark: ....

3. Julia said Stefan had been seasick on the ferry two weeks before.

   Julia: ....

4. The twins said they had not been able to go to Madame Tussaud's the day before.

   The twins: ....

5. Mr Johnson said the train had been late again.

   Mr Johnson: ....

Punkte: ☐ von 5

Lösungen Seite 114

Aufgabe 3 **Übersetze die Sätze ins Englische.**

1. Katies Eltern sagten ihr, dass sie nicht alleine einkaufen gehen könne.
2. Die Zwillinge sagten, dass sie das London Eye sehen wollten.
3. Julia schrieb ihrer Mutter, dass sie in London „Cats" gesehen hatte.
4. Stefan schrieb seiner Mutter, dass er das englische Essen nicht mag.
5. Julia sagte, dass Stefan jetzt besser in Englisch sei.
6. Mrs Johnson sagte ihrem Mann, dass die Zeit in London schön gewesen sei.

Punkte: ☐ von 12

Aufgabe 4 **Setze die Fragen in die direkte Rede.**

1. Mark asked when they could go to Madame Tussaud's.

....

2. Mandy asked if she could go shopping with Katie and Julia.

....

3. Mrs Johnson asked whether they wanted to see a musical.

....

4. Katie asked when they could go to the theatre.

....

5. Stefan asked whether he might go to the London Eye.

....

6. Mr Johnson asked when they had to return to Canterbury.

....

Punkte: ☐ von 6

Punkte: ☐ von 30

24–30: Bravo! Du weißt schon gut Bescheid.
16–23: Teilweise bist du sicher, teilweise noch nicht. Bearbeite noch einmal die Übungen, in denen du beim ersten Mal viele Fehler hattest.
0–15: Leider ist dir noch zu vieles unklar. Arbeite das Kapitel noch einmal durch.

Lösungen Seite 114

6

Satzformen

The Johnsons have decided to take Julia and Stefan to Edinburgh. As it is August, the Edinburgh Festival is taking place. The young people are not very interested in the concerts and the theatre, but they are really looking forward to the Tattoo, a performance by military bands playing the bagpipes and the drums. They hope to visit the Lake District on the way home and see the rocky scenery for themselves.

6.1 *Conditional Clauses (If-Clauses)*

Alles klar?! ***Conditional Clauses***

Bedingungssätze bestehen aus zwei Teilen:

If Julia stayed in Canterbury for some months,	*her English would be very good.*
einem Nebensatz (NS), der eine Bedingung angibt	einem Hauptsatz (HS), mit dem die Folge der Bedingung ausgedrückt wird
einleitende Konjunktion ***if*** (= wenn, falls)	(*then* = dann)

Hauptsatz und Nebensatz können vertauscht werden. Wenn der Hauptsatz an zweiter Stelle steht, wird meist ein Komma gesetzt.
Bedingungssätze (Typ II) drücken **Ereignisse** aus, die wahrscheinlich **nicht eintreten** werden, **Bedingungen**, die vermutlich **nicht erfüllt** werden.

Bei der Bildung ist auf die **Zeitformen** in **Haupt-** und **Nebensatz** zu achten:

***If*-Satz/Nebensatz**	**Hauptsatz**
*If Julia **stayed** in Canterbury for some months,*	*her English **would be** very good.*
simple past	conditional I

Merke

Noch einmal zur Erinnerung: Bedingungssätze (Typ I) drücken tatsächliche oder mögliche Ereignisse und Situationen in der Zukunft aus. Hier steht im *If*-Satz das Präsens und im Hauptsatz das Futur.

If Stefan goes to Scotland with the Johnsons, he will eat a lot of shortbread.

Präge dir folgende Tabelle gut ein:

	***If*-Satz/Nebensatz**	**Hauptsatz**
Typ I	**simple present**	**will-future**
Typ II	**simple past**	**conditional I**

Übung 1 **Setze die richtigen Verbformen für Konditionalsätze (Typ I) ein.**

1. If the Johnsons .... (to be) lucky, they .... (to get) tickets for the Tattoo.
2. If the young people .... (to go) to the Tattoo, Mr and Mrs Johnson .... (to go) to a concert.
3. Stefan .... (to be/not) pleased, if the bands .... (to play/ not) the bagpipes.
4. If Katie and Julia .... (to go) shopping, the twins .... (to book) a tour of Edinburgh.
5. If Stefan .... (to take) some photographs of Edinburgh, he .... (to be able) to show them to Jan.
6. Katie .... (to get) a headache, if the drummers .... (to stop/ not) playing soon.

Übung 2 ★ **Bilde Sätze mit *Conditional I*.**

1. If/they/to go/to Holyrood House/, they/to learn about/Mary Stuart.

....

2. If/they/to read/Schiller's play "Maria Stuart"/, they/to know/about her fate (= Schicksal).

....

3. If/he/to be a Scot/, Stefan/to love/to play the bagpipes.

....

4. Katie/to enjoy/the Scottish breakfast/if/she/to like/porridge.

....

5. If/the Johnsons/to hire/a car/, they/to be able/to tour the Highlands.

....

6. They/to be able/to see/the monster/if/they/to go/to Loch Ness.

....

Lösungen Seite 115

Übung 3 **Bilde Sätze aus den beiden Kästen.**

1. They will see a Celtic football match	if	he takes a photograph of Nessie
2. Her friends at home would laugh		Stefan and Mark visit Glasgow
3. Mr Johnson would go salmon fishing		Mrs Johnson liked biscuits
4. They will go shopping in Princes Street		Julia bought a kilt
5. He will play a game of golf		Katie could drive
6. Stefan will send it to a newspaper		he had enough time
7. She would buy a tin of shortbread		Katie and Julia get up early tomorrow
8. She would visit Balmoral		Mr Johnson goes to St Andrew's

1. ....
2. ....
3. ....
4. ....
5. ....
6. ....
7. ....
8. ....

Achtung
Kein *would* im *If*-Satz! Da in deutschen Konditionalsätzen sowohl im Haupt- wie im Nebensatz *würde* steht („Wenn Julia in England bleiben würde, würde ihr Englisch sehr gut werden"), muss man hier besonders gut aufpassen.
Also nicht einfach übersetzen, sondern immer an die Regel denken!

Lösungen Seite 115

6.2 *Adverbial Clauses*

Alles klar?! **Unterschiedliche Bedeutungen**

Mit Adverbialsätzen kann man, wie mit dem Adverbial, die näheren Umstände eines Geschehens – den Ort, die Zeit, den Grund … – genauer angeben.

Adverbialsätze haben verschiedene Bedeutungen:

Julia sees a lot of interesting things ***while*** *she is in Scotland with Katie.*	**Adverbialsätze der Zeit** *(adverbial clauses of time)*: temporal Frage: **Wann? Wie oft? Wie lange? Seit wann?** … **Einleitende Konjunktionen:** *when* (wenn, als), *after* (nachdem), *before* (bevor), *as soon as* (sobald), *till/until* (bis), *since* (seit), *while* (während)
Julia is looking forward to the trip ***because*** *Edinburgh is a beautiful city.*	**Adverbialsätze des Grundes** *(adverbial clauses of reason)*: kausal Frage: **Warum?** **Einleitende Konjunktionen:** *because* (weil), *as* (da)
Although *Julia doesn't understand everything, she enjoys herself very much.*	**Adverbialsätze der Einräumung/des Gegensatzes** *(adverbial clauses of concession)*: konzessiv Frage: **Trotz wessen?** **Einleitende Konjunktionen:** *although/though* (obwohl, obgleich), *while* (während), *even if* (selbst wenn)
Julia takes a lot of pictures ***so that*** *she can show them to her friends at home.*	**Adverbialsätze des Zwecks/der Folge** *(adverbial clauses of purpose)*: final Frage: **Wozu? Zu welchem Zweck?** **Einleitende Konjunktion:** *so/so that* (dass, damit)
If *Stefan goes to Edinburgh, he will hear the bagpipes.*	**Konditionalsatz** (Bedingung) (vgl. hierzu auch Seite 66 ff.) Frage: **Unter welcher Bedingung?** **Einleitende Konjunktion:** *if* (falls)
They go to the Castle ***where*** *they see the Tattoo.*	**Adverbialsätze des Ortes** *(adverbial clauses of place)*: lokal Frage: **Wo? Wohin? Woher?** … Der Lokalsatz stellt eine Besonderheit dar, da er nicht durch eine Konjunktion, sondern durch ein **Relativpronomen** eingeleitet wird. Er gehört also zu den Relativsätzen (vgl. hierzu auch Seite 71 ff.).

Bei Temporalsätzen mit *before* und *after* musst du die Zeitenfolge beachten.

After they had had breakfast, **past perfect**	*they went to the Castle.* **simple past**	**A vor B = vorzeitig**
Before they went to the Castle, **simple past**	*they had had breakfast.* **past perfect**	**A nach B = nachzeitig**

Übung 1 Markiere die richtige Konjunktion.

1. They stayed in their hotel until/so that it was time for the Tattoo.
2. They met for the Tattoo after/before they had been shopping.
3. They queued in the interval so that/before they could buy a drink.
4. Julia and Stefan could not join in when/although the audience sang "Scotland the Brave".
5. They didn't sing "Scotland the Brave" so/because they didn't know the words.
6. Although/Because they were tired, they went to a disco after the Tattoo.

Übung 2 Setze die Konjunktionen an der richtigen Stelle ein.

so that | *where* | *until* | *since* | *although* | *because*

Stefan has written to Jan about his stay in Britain.

1. .... I've been in Scotland, I've seen a lot of interesting sights.
2. We visited the Castle and stayed .... it closed.
3. We are leaving Edinburgh tomorrow .... we can visit the Lake District on the way home.
4. We might stop in Grasmere .... the Johnson's relatives live.
5. I would like to visit the Lake District .... I am fond of walking.
6. It will be fun to walk on the fells (Hügel) .... I haven't got my walking boots with me.

Lösungen Seite 115

6.3 Relative Clauses

Alles klar?! ***Defining Relative Clauses***

Julia showed Katie's friends some of the pictures ***which*** *she had taken in Germany.* *The boy* ***whom*** *she talked to at the club had been to Germany.*	**Relativsätze** werden in der Regel durch ein **Relativpronomen** eingeleitet. Das Relativpronomen verweist auf ein Nomen oder Pronomen, das im vorausgegangenen Satz verwendet wurde. Der Relativsatz macht so weitere Angaben zu den Nomen oder Pronomen. *Julia showed some of the pictures* ***which*** *she had taken of her friends.*
English is the subject ***that*** *Julia likes best.* *The boy* ***whose*** *mother is German talked to Julia about Germany.*	Relativpronomen im Englischen: *who(m)* verweist auf Personen *which* verweist auf Dinge oder Tiere *that* verweist auf Personen und Dinge *whose* verweist auf Personen und zeigt Besitzverhältnisse („wessen?")
	Bei den hier genannten Beispielen handelt es sich um **notwendige Relativsätze** ***(defining relative clauses)***. Sie sind zum Verständnis des Hauptsatzes notwendig und können deshalb nicht weggelassen werden. Sie werden nicht durch Komma vom Hauptsatz abgetrennt.
Julia showed Katie's friends some of the pictures she had taken in Germany. *The boy she talked to at the club had been to Germany.* *English is the subject Julia likes best.*	Besonders in der gesprochenen Sprache kann man die Relativpronomen *who, which, that* weglassen, wenn das Relativpronomen Objekt des Relativsatzes ist. Man spricht in diesem Fall von *contact clauses*.
The boy ***whom*** *she talked* ***to*** *had been to Germany.* *The boy she talked* ***to*** *had been to Germany.* *The CD* ***to which*** *Julia listened all the time was by her favourite group.*	Bei Verben mit Präpositionen kann die Präposition • bei den Relativpronomen *who(m), which, that* oder im *contact clause* im Anschluss an das Verb stehen, • bei den Relativpronomen *who(m), which, whose* **vor** dem Relativpronomen stehen.

Lerntipp

Whose oder *who's* klingen ähnlich, bedeuten aber etwas anderes.

Julia knows a boy whose father is German. (*Whose* ist hier Relativpronomen.)
Who's (= Who is) that boy? (*Who* ist hier Fragepronomen, *'s* steht für *is*.)
Who's (= Who has) got a calculator? (*Who* ist hier Fragepronomen, *'s* steht für *has*.)

Übung 1 **Setze die passenden Relativpronomen ein.**

1. The recorder .... Mandy has played for five years needs to be repaired.
2. The teacher .... taught my mother French is now teaching me.
3. The hotel .... the Johnsons had booked was near the Castle.
4. The music .... Stefan heard at the Tattoo was very loud.
5. The horse .... you saw yesterday was Little Richard.
6. The Lake District is one of the places in England .... tourists like to visit.

Übung 2 ★ **Schreibe in dein Heft die Sätze aus Übung 1, die *contact clauses* sind.**

Übung 3 **Verbinde die Sätze mit dem passenden Relativpronomen.**

1. The man was a Scot. Stefan spoke to the man.

....

2. The guide talked to Stefan. The guide's uniform was blue.

....

3. The band played the bagpipes. The band's members wore kilts.

....

4. The part of England was the Lake District. They wanted to go there.

....

5. The man was the conductor. They saw the man in front of the band.

....

6. The kilt was very expensive. Katie was looking at the kilt in the shop window.

....

Lösungen Seite 116

Alles klar?! ***Non-defining Relative Clauses***

Katie, <u>who really likes French</u>, enjoyed the French lesson very much.

Julia, <u>whose favourite subject is English</u>, really enjoyed the English lesson.

Neben den notwendigen gibt es auch **nicht notwendige Relativsätze *(non-defining relative clauses)***. Sie liefern zusätzliche Informationen, die für das Gesamtverständnis des Satzes nicht notwendig sind.

Diese Relativsätze werden mit Komma vom Hauptsatz abgetrennt.

Das Relativpronomen *that* kann hier nicht verwendet werden.

Übung 4 **Setze die passenden Relativpronomen ein.**

1. Mr Johnson, ... is keen to protect the environment, usually cycles to work.
2. Mark's football team, ... is one of the best in the school league, has just won the cup.
3. Stefan, ... grades in English have never been good, now finds English fun.
4. Mandy, to .... Mark is sometimes quite rude, can be very bossy.
5. Edinburgh Castle, ... the Johnsons enjoyed visiting, is at the top of a steep hill.
6. The monster, ... is said to live in Loch Ness, has hardly ever been seen.

Übung 5 ★ **Setze bei den nicht notwendigen Relativsätzen die Kommas ein.**

1. Many people who go to the Lake District want to walk on the fells.
2. The school choir which gives two concerts a year has learned three new songs.
3. Katie who loves riding is not sure whether she can afford any more lessons.
4. Mark who is very untidy has lost his football boots.
5. The boy who is brushing Little Richard is Anne's brother.
6. The dress which Julia is wearing was made by her mother.

Lösungen Seite 116

6.4 *Infinitives*

Alles klar?! Auf bestimmte Verben und Adjektive folgt der Infinitiv mit *to*.

Julia asked Mrs Johnson to help her.	Der Infinitiv steht nach bestimmten Verben und deren Objekt. Weitere Verben: *to allow* (erlauben), *to order* (befehlen), *to teach* (lehren/ beibringen), *to tell* (sagen)
For Julia it's easy to speak English.	Der Infinitiv steht nach bestimmten Adjektiven. Weitere Adjektive: *difficult* (schwierig), *hard* (hart), *right* (richtig), *wrong* (falsch/ unvernünftig)

Übung 1 Übersetze die Sätze ins Englische.

1. Julia bat Mrs Johnson, ihr zu helfen.
2. Julia findet es einfacher, Englisch zu sprechen.
3. Es ist manchmal schwierig für Katie, Deutsch zu verstehen.
4. Sein Vater hat Mark das Schwimmen beigebracht.
5. Es ist falsch, im Lake District ohne Wanderstiefel zu wandern.
6. Ihre Eltern haben es den Zwillingen erlaubt, nach dem Tattoo in die Disco zu gehen.

1. ....

2. ....

3. ....

4. ....

5. ....

6. ....

 Lösungen Seite 117

Abschlusstest (30 Minuten)

Aufgabe 1 **Finde den Fehler und setze die richtige Form ein.**

1. If Stefan would work harder, he would get better grades.

....

2. If Katie has more lessons, she would be a better rider.

....

3. They will see lakes and mountains if they went to the Highlands.

....

4. If they would walk on the fells, they would be fit.

....

5. If it rains at the Tattoo tomorrow, they would get wet.

....

6. Mr Johnson will move to the Lake District if he could retire.

....

Punkte: ☐ von 6

Aufgabe 2 **Übersetze ins Englische.**

1. Nachdem sie in der Disco waren, gingen sie ins Hotel zurück.
2. Sie verließen Edinburgh am Abend, damit sie einen ganzen Tag im Lake District verbringen (to spend) konnten.
3. Sie wollten zum Lake District fahren, weil die Johnsons dort Verwandte hatten.
4. Während die jungen Leute beim Tattoo waren, gingen Mr und Mrs Johnson ins Konzert.
5. Sie gingen nicht zum Tattoo, weil es ihnen zu laut war.
6. Sie besuchten Holyrood House, wo sie viel über das Leben Maria Stuarts erfuhren.

Punkte: ☐ von 12

Aufgabe 3 **Bilde Adverbialsätze mit den folgenden Satzteilen. Benutze die passenden Konjunktionen, achte auf die Zeiten.**

1. Mr Johnson/to cycle/to work/helmet/to put on/always.

....

2. Stefan/to not like/the English breakfast/at first/he/now/to enjoy/it.

....

Lösungen Seite 117

3. They/to have/a drink/time/to be/in the bar/for the concert.

....

4. The twins/to try to speak/very clearly/Stefan/to be able to/to understand/them.

....

5. We/to have to/to hurry/to the Castle/it/to close/at 6 pm.

....

6. Stefan/to write/his postcards/to be/in/the Lake District.

....

Punkte: ☐ von 6

Aufgabe 4 **Verbessere die Relativpronomen, eventuell auch die Reihenfolge.**

1. That's the boy which Mark sits next to at school.

....

2. This is the cousin that's family lives in the Lake District.

....

3. That is the horse on that Katie rides.

....

4. This is the programme about horses to whom Katie listens every day.

....

5. That is the guide which Stefan spoke to.

....

6. That is the waitress which Mr Johnson gave the large tip to.

....

Punkte: ☐ von 6

Punkte: ☐ von 30

24–30: Bravo! Du weißt schon gut Bescheid.
16–23: Teilweise bist du sicher, teilweise noch nicht. Bearbeite noch einmal die Übungen, in denen du beim ersten Mal viele Fehler hattest.
0–15: Leider ist dir noch zu vieles unklar. Arbeite das Kapitel noch einmal durch.

Lösungen Seite 117

7

Textverständnis

The Johnsons had planned to go to the Highlands after their stay in Edinburgh, but they went to the Lake District instead because there was not enough time for them to travel the extra 500 kilometres to the Highlands and back. Stefan was sad; he once read an article about the Loch Ness monster which captured his imagination. He had secretly hoped that they would arrive just at the time when Nessie made one of her rare appearances. One click of his camera and he would be rich and famous! In this chapter you will read the article that Stefan read and you can decide for yourself how likely it is that Stefan's dream will ever come true.

7.1 *Understanding a Text*

Fact or fiction?

Nessie is said to live in Scotland's Loch Ness (Loch is the Gaelic word for lake), which is in the Scottish Highlands, 37 kilometres southwest of Inverness, and is in one place extremely deep at 230 metres. No one has ever been able to prove that the Loch Ness monster actually exists or to establish what kind of animal it might be. Nessie would quite possibly never have become the cause of so much interest and speculation if a new road had not been built in 1933 alongside the remote lake. The first sighting followed shortly afterwards when George Spicer and his wife saw 'a most extraordinary form of animal' cross the road in front of their car. They described the creature as having a large body about 1 metre high and 8 metres long and a long, narrow neck, slightly thicker than an elephant's trunk and as long as 3.0 to 3.7 metres, the width of the road; the neck had a number of undulations (= wellenähnliche Form) in it. They saw no legs because of a dip in the road, which hid the lower part of the animal's body. It crawled across the road towards the loch 20 metres away, leaving only a trail of broken branches behind it.

In August 1933 a motorcyclist named Arthur Grant claimed to have nearly hit the creature on a moonlit night. Grant saw a small head attached to a long neck; the creature saw him and crossed the road back into the loch. Grant got off his bike and followed it to the loch, but only saw traces of movement in the water. However, some believe this was only a joke by a friend of Grant.

A photograph taken in 1935 and published in the Daily Mail was initially considered to prove the existence of Nessie; it showed a creature with a head and neck, but it later turned out to be a trick. The photograph was, in fact, of a toy submarine with a head and neck attached made of plastic wood and the aim was to annoy the newspaper, which had made fun of one of its writers in an article. Sporadic land sightings continued until 1963, when a poor-quality film of the creature was made from a distance of several miles.

On May 26, 2007, Gordon Holmes, a 55-year-old laboratory technician, produced a video of what he said was "this black thing, about 14 metres long, swimming fairly fast in the water." Adrian Shine, a marine biologist at the Loch Ness 2000 centre in Drumnadrochit, has watched the video and suggested that the footage in fact showed an otter, seal or water bird.

There have been a number of searches for the monster involving sonar equipment and underwater cameras, but they have neither been able to prove nor disprove the existence of an unknown creature in Loch Ness. Many attempts have been made over the years to explain the numerous sightings. These may be categorized as: an unknown species of large animal; a mystic or paranormal phenomenon; a misidentification of known animals; an inanimate object, such as a tree trunk, or a trick. It is worth noting that most sightings are of a large shape in the water; very few give any detailed descriptions. In addition, so far there has not been any physical evidence of the creature, such as skeletal remains, the capture of a live animal, tissue samples, tracks or trails. But for those who are convinced of Nessie's existence this does not prove anything at all.

Übung 1 **Read the text and find the answers to the following questions.**

a) What kind of text is it? Is it a letter, a story, a report …?
b) What is the subject of the text?

The title and keywords will help you to get a general impression. Read the text a second time and underline the keywords, then make notes on the keywords. See if you can identify some of the words you don't know from the context.

Übung 2 ★ **Fact or fiction? Have a closer look at the first sighting of Nessie.**

a) Answer the questions: Who? What? Where? When? How?

....

....

....

....

b) Do you think that this is a true story? Give reasons and answer in complete sentences.

....

....

....

....

c) Do you think that Stefan will ever get a picture of Nessie? Give reasons.

....

....

....

....

Lösungen Seite 118

Übung 3 **Read the text again and answer the following questions.**

a) Where is Loch Ness situated?

....

b) Why did Nessie become the cause of interest?

....

c) When did the first sighting happen?

....

d) What did Arthur Grant claim?

....

e) What trick was played on the Daily Mail and why?

....

f) What has been done to find Nessie?

....

g) How have some of the sightings been explained?

....

h) Why are some people not convinced of Nessie's existence?

....

Übung 4 **Read the text. Underline all the words you can find which belong to the word field of *movement*. List them and add some of your own.**

Übung 5 **Word families: find the verb related to the following nouns.**

life	....	suggestion	....
building	....	attempt	....
description	....	explanation	....
proof	....	remains	....

Lösungen Seite 118

Übung 6 **Why did Stefan's dream not come true? Complete the story in your own words.**

Although Stefan was disappointed that they could not go to the Highlands, he understood why the Johnson's had made the decision.

From Edinburgh .... way, the journey ....
.... Mr and Mrs Johnson also wanted ....
.... who live in the .... .They had .... for a very long time. The twins wanted to .... on the fells. Stefan was disappointed because the story of Nessie ....
and he had hoped .... of Nessie ....
.... appearances and he had also hoped ....
.... and send .... to .... to make him ......
.... He decided .... return some time in the future to .... to .... for himself and see ....
.... He is quite certain that ....
only person to .... that there really .... in the lake.

Lösungen Seite 119

Abschlusstest (25 Minuten)

Aufgabe 1 **Find the opposites.**

1. shallow ....
2. first ....
3. in front of ....
4. narrow ....
5. thick ....
6. upper ....
7. unknown ....
8. finally ....

Punkte: ☐ von 8

Aufgabe 2 **Use your dictionary to find the meaning of the words and translate the expressions into German.**

1. to become the cause of interest ....
2. the width of the road ....
3. remote ....
4. the trail of broken branches ....
5. traces of movement in the water ....
6. the first sighting of Nessie ....
7. turned out to be a trick ....
8. the aim was to annoy ....
9. an inanimate object ....
10. it is worth noting ....

Punkte: ☐ von 10

Lösungen Seite 119

Aufgabe 3 **Collocations: put the most suitable adjective with the noun.**

1. shallow	discussion
2. fictitious	experience
3. frightening	story
4. lively	proof
5. convincing	attempt
6. successful	water

Punkte: ☐ von 6

Punkte: ☐ von 24

19–24: Bravo! Du weißt schon gut Bescheid.
13–18: Teilweise bist du sicher, teilweise noch nicht. Bearbeite noch einmal die Übungen, in denen du beim ersten Mal viele Fehler hattest.
0–12: Leider ist dir noch zu vieles unklar. Arbeite das Kapitel noch einmal durch.

Lösungen Seite 119

8

Wortschatz und Situationen

Learning words is boring? Well, maybe. But learning words can also be fun.
On the next pages you'll find some ideas to make learning words more interesting, exciting, a game with your friends …
When you are learning words for school next time, just have a look at the following pages and use some of the ideas – and you'll see: learning words will be a lot easier.

8.1 Den Wortschatz sichern und erweitern

Alles klar?! **Mehr Spaß beim Lernen mit Spielen**

Vokabeln kannst du sehr gut üben, wenn du mit Freunden zusammen bist. Dann könnt ihr euch Rätsel überlegen, die die anderen lösen, oder Spiele, die ihr gemeinsam spielt. Hier zwei Beispiele für solche lustigen Lernspiele:

Explaining words

- Das ist ein Spiel, das mit mehreren Mitspielern gespielt werden muss.
- Bastelt Kärtchen, auf die ihr einen Begriff schreibt, den die Mitspieler erklären sollen.
- Zu diesem Begriff ergänzt ihr weitere Wörter, die bei Erklärungen nicht verwendet werden dürfen, z. B.

children	**school**	**parents**
• school • parents • to play • young	• to learn • teacher • class • children	• children • mother • father • at home

- Bildet zwei Gruppen: A und B. Eine Person aus Gruppe A erklärt/umschreibt das fett gedruckte Wort, ohne die anderen Wörter zu benutzen. Der Rest der Gruppe A rät.
- Gruppe B kontrolliert, ob die Wörter, die nicht verwendet werden dürfen, auch wirklich nicht verwendet wurden. Wenn sie verwendet wurden, bekommt Gruppe B die Karte und somit einen Punkt.
- Nach einer Minute wechselt ihr. Nun erklärt eine Person aus Gruppe B das fett gedruckte Wort, und Gruppe B muss raten.
- Die Gruppe, die nach ca. zehn Minuten mehr Karten geraten hat, ist Sieger.

Lösungen Seite 120

Alles klar?! **Odd man out**

Um hier Rätsel für deine Freundin/deinen Freund zu erstellen, kannst du Wortreihen zugrunde legen, die du zum Lernen von Wörtern bildest (vgl. Seite 87). Mische ein Wort darunter, das nicht so gut passt, und deine Freundin/dein Freund muss herausfinden, welches Wort das ist, d. h., sie/er muss den „odd man" – den Außenseiter – finden.

Übung 1 **Streiche den „odd man" durch.**

- to see, to listen, to taste, to smell, to feel
- to walk, to run, to crawl, to sit
- to cycle, to run, to drive, to go by train
- second, minute, hour, day, clock

Alles klar?! **Leichter lernen mit Wortpartnern**

Wörter kannst du dir besser merken, wenn du sie mit „Partnern", d. h. Wörtern, die eng zu ihnen gehören, zusammen lernst. Besonders geeignet sind dafür Gegensatzpaare oder Wortreihen.

Wortreihen kannst du zum Beispiel aus Wörtern bilden, die zusammengehören:
- Sinneswahrnehmungen: *to see, to hear, to taste, to smell, to feel*
- Fortbewegungsmöglichkeiten: *to walk, to run, to crawl, to skip*
- Fortbewegung mit Verkehrsmitteln: *to cycle, to drive, to go by train, to go by bus*
- Zeiteinheiten: *second, minute, hour, day, week, month, year*

Lösungen Seite 120

Übung 2 **Ergänze den fehlenden Partner, sodass du ein Gegensatzpaar erhältst.**

- **bei Adjektiven**

clean –	....	high –	....
difficult –	....	poor –	....
happy –	....	possible –	....
healthy –	....	slow –	....

- **bei Nomen**

day –	....	spring –	....
morning –	....	summer –	....

- **bei Verben**

to arrive –	....	to hurry up –	....
to finish –	....	to laugh –	....
to hate –	....	to start –	....

- **bei Adverbien**

always –	....	late –	....
indoors –	....	sometimes –	....

Übung 3 **Verbinde die Wörter, die zusammengehören.**

to go	a trip	....
to go to	by bus	....
to plan	English	....
to practise	London	....
to visit	places	....

Lösungen Seite 120

8.2 Arbeit mit dem Wörterbuch

Alles klar?! **Wörter verstehen – mit und ohne Wörterbuch**

Nicht alle Wörter kannst du auswendig kennen, manchmal musst du natürlich Wörter auch nachschlagen. Für den Moment solltest du dir ein mittelgroßes zweisprachiges Wörterbuch anschaffen.

Dennoch kannst du Texte verstehen, ohne dass du alle Wörter kennst. Bevor du ein Wort nachschlägst, solltest du versuchen, es zu erschließen:

- Der **Kontext**, in dem das Wort steht, gibt dir manchmal wichtige Hinweise.
- Vielleicht findest du ein **Bild** bei dem Text, das dir helfen könnte, das Wort zu verstehen.
- Vielleicht liefert dir ein verwandtes englisches Wort oder ein **ähnliches Wort** aus dem Deutschen oder einer anderen Sprache Hinweise darauf, was das unbekannte Wort bedeuten könnte. Aber Vorsicht vor „falschen Freunden".
- Denke aber auch daran, dass man nicht jedes Wort kennen muss, um einen Text zu verstehen.

Und wenn das alles nichts hilft? Kein Problem – denn dafür gibt es ja **Wörterbücher**!

In einem guten Wörterbuch findest du je nach Stichwort folgende Informationen:

1. eine oder oft auch mehrere **Übersetzungen** des Worts, ggf. getrennt nach unterschiedlichen Bedeutungen,
2. **Anwendungsbeispiele** wie idiomatische Wendungen, feste Verbindungen mit anderen Wörtern oder sogar ganze Beispielsätze,
3. Angaben zur **Grammatik**, zum **Sprachgebrauch**, zu Unterschieden zwischen britischem und amerikanischem Englisch,
4. die **Aussprache** in internationaler Lautschrift (bei elektronischen Wörterbüchern für den PC oder im Internet kannst du dir viele Stichwörter auch vorsprechen lassen),
5. manchmal sogar weitere **Verständnishilfen** wie Zeichnungen, Fotos oder Infokästen mit zusätzlichen Informationen.

Alles klar?! Richtig nachschlagen im Wörterbuch

Wörterbücher bieten dir viele praktische Hilfen, damit du das gesuchte Wort schnell findest.

100

child

C

child [tʃaɪld] ⚠ *Pl.*: **children** ['tʃɪldrən] Kind; ***be a good child!*** sei artig *oder* brav!; ***that's child's play*** *übertragen* das ist ein Kinderspiel
childbirth ['tʃaɪldbɜːθ] Geburt, Entbindung
childhood ['tʃaɪldhʊd] Kindheit; ***from childhood*** von Kindheit an
childish ['tʃaɪldɪʃ] **1.** kindlich **2.** *Erwachsener*: kindisch
childlike ['tʃaɪldlaɪk] kindlich
childminder ['tʃaɪld,maɪndə] *BE* Tagesmutter
childproof ['tʃaɪldpruːf] kindersicher; ***childproof lock*** *Auto*: Kindersicherung
children ['tʃɪldrən] *Pl. von* → **child**; ***children's home*** Kinderheim
child seat ['tʃaɪld_siːt] *Auto*: Kindersitz
chill¹ [tʃɪl] **1.** kühlen (*Getränk usw.*) **2.** ***chilled to the bone*** *Person*: (völlig) durchgefroren
chill² [tʃɪl] **1.** Erkältung; ***catch a chill*** sich erkälten **2.** Kälte (*auch übertragen*); ***take the chill off something*** etwas leicht anwärmen
chill³ [tʃɪl] *auch* ***chill out*** relaxen
chilly ['tʃɪlɪ] kalt, frostig (*auch übertragen*)
chime¹ [tʃaɪm] **1.** (Glocken)Schlag **2.** *oft* ***chimes*** *Pl.* Glockenspiel
chime² [tʃaɪm] **1.** (*Glocken*) läuten, (*Uhr*) schlagen
chimney ['tʃɪmnɪ] Schornstein, Kamin
chimney-piece ['tʃɪmnɪpiːs] Kaminsims
chimney-sweep ['tʃɪmnɪswiːp] Schornsteinfeger(in), Kaminkehrer(in)

chimpanzee [⚠ ,tʃɪmpæn'ziː] *umg. auch* ***chimp*** Schimpanse
chin [tʃɪn] **1.** Kinn **2.** (***keep your***) ***chin up!*** *umg.* Kopf hoch!, halt die Ohren steif!
China ['tʃaɪnə] China
china ['tʃaɪnə] **1.** Porzellan **2.** *auch* ***chinaware*** Porzellan(geschirr)
Chinatown ['tʃaɪnətaʊn] Chinatown, Chinesenviertel
Chinese¹ [,tʃaɪ'niːz] chinesisch
Chinese² [,tʃaɪ'niːz] *Sprache*: Chinesisch
Chinese³ [,tʃaɪ'niːz] Chinese, Chinesin; ***the Chinese*** *Pl.* die Chinesen
chink¹ [tʃɪŋk] Riss, Ritze, Spalt
chink² [tʃɪŋk] **1.** klirren, klimpern **2.** klirren *oder* klimpern mit
chinwag¹ ['tʃɪnwæg] *bes. BE, umg.* Plauderei, Plausch
chinwag² ['tʃɪnwæg] *bes. BE, umg.* plaudern, plauschen
chip¹ [tʃɪp] **1.** *an Tasse, Teller usw.*: angeschlagene Stelle **2.** *von Holz usw.*: Splitter, Span **3.** ***chips*** *Pl. BE* ⚠ Pommes frites **4.** ***chips*** *Pl. AE* ⚠ (Kartoffel)Chips **5.** *beim Roulette usw.*: Chip, Spielmarke **6.** *Elektrotechnik*: Chip

chips

Achte auf den Unterschied

Englisch	Deutsch
BE **chips**	Pommes frites
AE **(potato) chips**	Kartoffelchips

Deutsch	Englisch
Kartoffelchips	*BE* **crisps**, *AE* **(potato) chips**
Pommes frites	*BE* **chips**, *AE* **(French) fries**

Übrigens: Auch in britischen Restaurants werden Pommes frites oft als **French fries** bzw. **French fried potatoes** bezeichnet.

chip² [tʃɪp], ***chipped, chipped*** anschlagen (*Geschirr usw.*)

chip in [,tʃɪp'ɪn] *umg.* **1.** *im Gespräch*: einwerfen (*Bemerkung usw.*) **2.** sich einmischen (*in ein Gespräch*) **3.** beisteuern (*Geld usw.*)
chip off [,tʃɪp'ɒf] abbrechen, abbröckeln

Übung 1 **Löse die folgenden Aufgaben mithilfe der Wörterbuchabbildung.**

When Tom was in London, he ate chips every day.

a) Schlage das Wort *chip* aus dem obigen Satz nach. (Die entsprechende Seite ist gegenüber schon aufgeschlagen.) Wo auf dieser Seite stehen die Informationen, die dir das Nachschlagen erleichtern, und wie lauten sie hier?

nach dem Stichwort | obere äußere Seitenecke | alphabetisch richtige Stelle | Seitenrand

Informationen	**Wo stehen sie?**	**Wie lauten sie hier?**
Buchstabe im Alphabet		
blaues Leitwort		
blaues Stichwort		
Hochzahl		

Mit so vielen Hilfen ist es doch ganz einfach, das Wort zu finden, das du suchst! Nun möchtest du ja aber auch noch wissen, was ***chips*** in dem Satz oben bedeutet – und die erste Übersetzung ist nicht immer die richtige Übersetzung! Moderne und gute Wörterbücher zeigen dir genau, in welchem Zusammenhang ein Wort vorkommen kann. Schau dir deshalb zu jeder Bedeutung (Ziffern 1. bis 6.) auch die *kursiven* Erklärungen an!

b) Schreibe hinter jede Zahl eine Bedeutung des Wortes **chip** aus dem Wörterbuch. Worauf kann sich die jeweilige Bedeutung beziehen? Fallen dir für „usw." noch andere Beispiele ein als die, die im Wörterbuch angegeben sind?

TIPP: Ein Warndreieck ⚠ bedeutet: „Vorsicht! Hier kann man etwas verwechseln!"

1. ....

2. ....

3. ....

4. ....

5. ....

6. ....

c) Wie heißt der Satz also auf Deutsch?

When Tom was in London, he ate chips every day.

....

Die Zeichnungen und der blaue Kasten im Wörterbuch zeigen dir nochmal ausführlich, was der Unterschied zwischen *chips* in Großbritannien und *chips* in den USA ist.

Lösungen Seite 121

8.3 Situationen meistern

Alles klar?! ***Situations: Going shopping/*****Einkaufen gehen**

Für bestimmte Situationen ist es gut, wenn man nicht nur die Wörter kann, sondern sich feststehende Wendungen merkt. Hier findest du nützliche Redewendungen fürs Einkaufen.

Shop assistant	**Shopper**
	Excuse me, could you please help me? Excuse me, where can I find …? Excuse me, I can't find the … .
Good morning. Can I help you?	Yes, please. I'm looking for … Do you have … No, thank you, I'm just looking around.
How do you like …? What is your size? Well, I'm sorry we don't have …	Could I please try this/these … on? This is too big/small. Have you got a smaller/bigger size? I'm afraid this is too expensive for me. Do you have something cheaper? I don't like this so much. Could you show me something else? I have to think about it. I think I'll have to look somewhere else then.
It is (five pounds twenty-five)./They are (ten pounds fifty.)	How much is/are …? That's too expensive for me. I'll take it. Thanks, that's all.

British money

Als Währungseinheit haben die Briten das Pfund = *pound*, das Symbol dafür ist: £. £1 = 100 pence, abgekürzt „p“, ausgesprochen [pens].
Das Symbol (£) wird immer vor dem Preis geschrieben: *£1.20; £4.25.*
Man sagt allerdings: *one pound twenty, four pounds (Plural!) twenty-five.*

Übung 1 **Bringe den Dialog in die richtige Reihenfolge. Unterstreiche anschließend Ausdrücke, die beim Einkaufen wichtig sind.**

Julia: £10? Ok, I'll take it.
Julia: Hmm, not so much really. I don't like the colours. This pink is really shocking. Could you show me something else? How about those over there? They look really cool.
Julia: I think small is fine. It looks great. ... How much is it?
Julia: Yes, please. I'm looking for a new T-shirt.

Shop assistant: Good morning. Can I help you?
Shop assistant: It's £10.
Shop assistant: Let's see. We've got some nice ones over there. Have a look. Young people like them very much. How do you like them?
Shop assistant: Would you like to try one on? What's your size?

Shop assistant: ....

Julia: ....

Shop assistant: ....

....

Julia: ....

....

Shop assistant: ....

Julia: ....

Shop assistant: ....

Julia: ....

Lösungen Seite 122

Übung 2 ★ **Ergänze die Lücken.**

Shop assistant: Good morning. ....?

Katie: Yes, please. .... a pair of sandals.

Shop assistant: Let's see. We've got some nice ones over there. Have a look. .... them?

Katie: Hmm, not so much really. The style is nice, but I wanted red ones. Have you got those in red?

Shop assistant: No, I'm sorry. But how about those over there?

Katie: Ahh … they look really cool. And I like the colour very much.

Shop assistant: Would you ....? .... your size?

Katie: I think size 6 is fine. But could you tell me first .... they are?

Shop assistant: They are £35.

Katie: £35! .... for me. I'll have to ask my mother first.

Shop assistant: Well, I'm sorry, but we don't have any cheaper ones.

Katie: Well, thank you. I think I'll have to look somewhere else then. Good bye.

Shop assistant: Good bye.

Colours und patterns/Farben und Muster

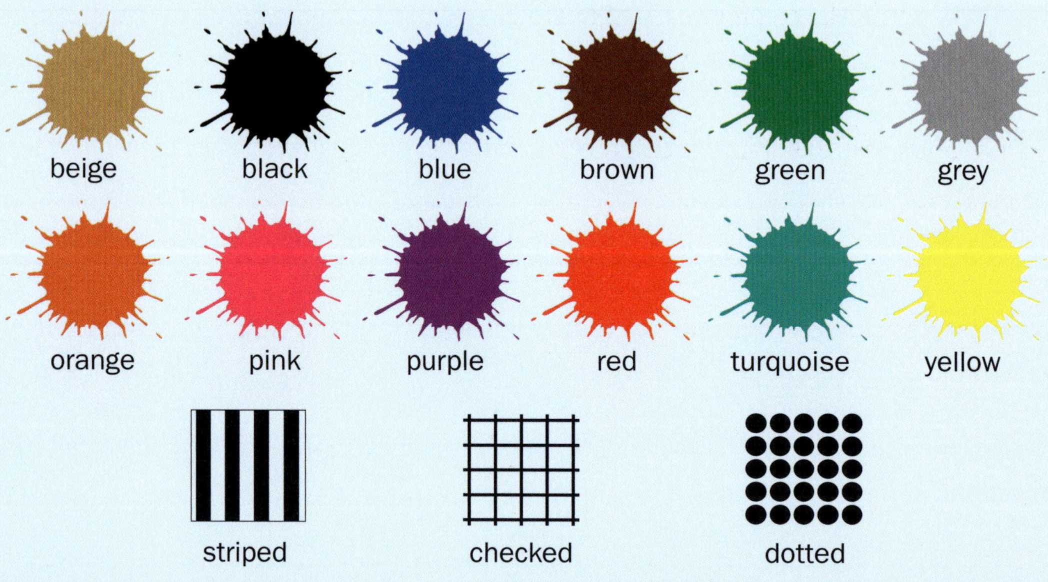

Lösungen Seite 122

Abschlusstest (25 Minuten)

Aufgabe 1 **Ergänze die Gegensätze.**

1. cheap – ....
2. dark – ....
3. exciting – ....
4. friendly – ....
5. big – ....
6. long – ....
7. successful – ....
8. usual – ....

Punkte: ☐ von 8

Aufgabe 2 **Wann sagst du folgende Sätze, wenn du beim Einkaufen bist.**

1. Excuse me, could you please help me? ☐
2. I'm looking for an interesting, not so difficult book. ☐
3. Could I please try these shoes on? ☐
4. They are too small. Have you got a bigger size? ☐
5. I'm afraid this is too expensive for me. Do you have something cheaper? ☐

a) Du fragst, ob du die Schuhe anprobieren kannst.
b) Du bittest um Hilfe.
c) Du sagst, dass die Schuhe zu klein sind, und fragst, ob sie ein größeres Paar haben.
d) Du fragst nach einem interessanten, nicht so schwierigen Buch.
e) Du sagst, dass etwas zu teuer für dich ist, und fragst, ob es etwas Billigeres gibt.

Punkte: ☐ von 5

Lösungen Seite 122/123

Aufgabe 3 **Wie sagst du Folgendes auf Englisch?**

1. Du sagst, dass du dich nur umschauen willst.

....

2. Du bittest darum, dass man dir etwas anderes zeigt.

....

3. Du fragst, wie viel das T-Shirt kostet.

....

4. Du sagst, dass du es kaufst.

....

5. Du bedankst dich und verabschiedest dich.

....

Punkte: ☐ von 10

Punkte: ☐ von 23

19–23: Bravo! Du weißt schon gut Bescheid.
12–18: Teilweise bist du sicher, teilweise noch nicht. Bearbeite noch einmal die Übungen, in denen du beim ersten Mal viele Fehler hattest.
0–11: Leider ist dir noch zu vieles unklar. Arbeite das Kapitel noch einmal durch.

Lösungen Seite 123

Lösungen

1.1 Revision: *Simple Present, Present Perfect, Simple Past* und *Past Progressive*

Übung 1 (Seite 7)

1. The Grüners live in Osnabrück.
2. They have lived there for six years.
3. Julia usually goes to school by bike.
4. The cycle ride to school takes 20 minutes.
5. Today her father has taken her by car.
6. This morning she has arrived in school early.

Übung 2 (Seite 7)

1. Before they moved to Osnabrück, the Grüners lived in Cologne.
2. Yesterday Thomas broke his leg.
3. Mark is sad, because he has lost his football.
4. Katie sent Julia a present for her birthday last week.
5. Mandy has just finished her homework.
6. Jan bought a new computer game on the way home from school.

Übung 3 (Seite 7)

Julia is 16 years old and her brother Stefan, who is 13 years old, both live with their parents in Osnabrück. They have both attended the local grammar school since they were ten years old. Stefan does not like foreign languages, but Julia has had an English pen friend for 3 years. Two years ago she visited her friend Katie in Canterbury. She enjoyed herself very much and hopes to return soon. Stefan has never been abroad; he prefers to spend his holidays camping with friends. While Julia visited Katie, Stefan had a holiday beside a lake in Bavaria. Julia tries to send an email to Katie every week and Katie always replies immediately. They plan to spend another holiday together when they have passed their tests at the end of the school year.

Übung 4 (Seite 8)

1. What was Julia doing when Stefan entered the room?
2. Julia finished her letter, then she did her homework.
3. While Stefan was watching/watched TV, Julia was phoning/phoned Mary.
4. Stefan and his friends were playing football when it started to rain.
5. Stefan picked up the ball and ran home as quickly as possible.
6. Stefan and Julia ate their supper before they went to the cinema.

1.2 *Present Perfect Progressive*

Übung 1 (Seite 9)

1. Stefan has never been to England.
2. Julia has been writing a letter to her penfriend all morning.
3. Mother has prepared the lunch, but Julia has not set the table.
4. Stefan has been camping in Bavaria since last Tuesday.
5. Julia and Stefan have lived in Osnabrück for six years.
6. Julia has been learning English for four years.

Übung 2 (Seite 10)

Every summer for the past five years Julia and Stefan's parents, Mr and Mrs Grüner, have had a barbecue in their garden for friends and neighbours. Last year, just when everyone was having a good time, it started to rain heavily. All the guests rushed inside, but Julia and Stefan tried to carry as much indoors as they could. While Stefan was picking up all the glasses and dishes, Julia was taking plates of food into the kitchen. When no one was looking, the family dog, Benno, ate a large number of sausages. This year the Grüner family have decided to hire a large tent. They want to stay dry however bad the weather is, and they also hope that Benno, who without doubt has been dreaming of sausages ever since, will not eat as many as last year.

1.3 *Past Perfect/Past Perfect Progressive*

Übung 1 (Seite 12)

1. After Stefan had played tennis, he had a shower.
2. When the guests had arrived, Mr Grüner switched on all the lights.
3. As soon as Julia had written a letter, she went to the post-box.
4. After the lightning had struck the house, it caught fire.
5. Before Benno had finished all the sausages, he fell asleep.
6. As soon as the teacher had written the questions, the pupils started work.

Übung 2 (Seite 13)

1. When the train finally drew into the station, the passengers had been waiting for twenty minutes.
2. Benno had already eaten seven sausages when the twins found him under the table.
3. The Grüners had always invited friends to a party in their house, but last year they had a barbecue in the garden.
4. Mr Grüner had been worrying for some time about the weather and decided to hire a tent.
5. When Julia had been learning English for three years, she had the chance of getting an English penfriend.
6. Stefan had never wanted to learn a foreign language, but he quite liked English.

Übung 3 (Seite 13)

1. Stefan had been playing tennis for two hours when rain stopped play.
2. The doorbell finally rang one hour after Mrs Grüner had ordered the taxi.
3. Katie was late for her riding lesson, because she had been talking on the phone for hours.
4. Ben's knee hurt after he had fallen down on the football pitch.
5. After they had been living in Cologne for eight years they moved to Osnabruck.
6. The teacher gave the class extra work after they had been laughing and shouting all morning.

1.4 *Future*

Übung 1 (Seite 15)

1. The carnival procession will take place next week.
2. My daughter is going to be a princess in the procession.
3. Hundreds of people will cheer as the procession goes past.
4. I am sure they will enjoy themselves.
5. It's already late, I am going to find us a place with a good view of the procession.
6. With the streets so full of people you are going to find it difficult to get to the station.

Übung 2 (Seite 15)

1. The Grüners are having a party tonight. It starts at 6 pm.
2. I am sure that we will have a good view of the procession from here.
3. What will he be doing this time tomorrow?
4. Hurry up! It is after 6 o'clock and we will be late.
5. The procession leaves the town hall at 2 pm.

Abschlusstest

Aufgabe 1 (Seite 16)

1. Stefan has liked camping since he was six.
2. Stefan wants to go camping with his friend Jan in the Easter holidays.
3. Jan has never been camping before.
4. Stefan has told him what fun camping is.
5. Last time Stefan and his friends took their bikes with them.
6. Jan's parents have allowed him to go camping with Stefan and his friends.

Aufgabe 2 (Seite 16)

1. While the other boys were putting up the tent, Stefan and Thomas fetched water from the nearby farm.
2. When Stefan and Thomas returned to the camp, the others unpacked/were unpacking the food.
3. While the water was boiling, everyone helped to prepare the meal.
4. They were eating their meal when it started raining.
5. When the rain stopped, the boys washed the dishes and then played a game of football.
6. While they were playing football, the farmer arrived with some fresh eggs.

Aufgabe 3 (Seite 17)

1. Katie has been learning German for four years.
2. She has just written a long letter to Julia about her trip to Folkestone.
3. Has Jan gone to school today?
4. Stefan has done/has been doing his homework, but Julia has been helping/has helped their mother.
5. Stefan and Jan have spent a week at the camp.
6. Mr Grüner has been cleaning the barbecue all morning.

Aufgabe 4 (Seite 17)

1. The boys had been camping for a week when their parents came to fetch them.
2. How long had you been waiting for her when she phoned you?
3. Thomas had never liked English until he spent a holiday in London.
4. Jan had been playing computer games for hours when his mother arrived home from work.
5. When she was a child, Katie had learned the piano.
6. Ever since she was six years old, Katie had wanted to have a horse.

Aufgabe 5 (Seite 18)

1. Look at the lovely blue sky; it is going to be a fine day.
2. Julia is planning to visit Katie next year.
3. The bus to Canterbury leaves at 6 pm.
4. When she has finished her homework, Julia will write to Katie.
5. When I leave school, I am going to become a teacher.
6. Next year Julia will be visiting Katie.

Aufgabe 6 (Seite 18)

On Julia's first visit to England two years ago, she spent all the time with Katie in Canterbury. While she was there, they discussed her next visit. Now Julia is making definite plans. She hopes to see more of the country this time. She has been looking at travel brochures and has decided which places she wants to see. She is leaving for Britain at the end of term and is spending/is going to spend/will spend four weeks with Katie. They are going to visit/will visit/will be visiting London, of course, but Julia is also planning a trip to other parts of the UK. She had hoped to visit Northern Ireland, but has found out that there will not be enough time. She will definitely visit/is definitely going to visit York and Edinburgh. This means that she will see at least two of the countries of the UK.

2.1 Modale Hilfsverben *can/could/to be able to/to be allowed to*

Übung 1 (Seite 21)

Julia:	Can Stefan and I stay with you in Canterbury?
Katie:	Yes, you can.
Julia:	Can the twins look after Stefan?
Katie:	Yes, they can. But can't he look after himself?
Julia:	Oh, yes he can. I meant: could the twins show Stefan the sights and talk to him in English?
Katie:	Of course, they could. Will he be able to speak a lot of English?
Julia:	No, he won't. He could only speak very little English when we went to Malta last year.
Katie:	But Stefan will be able to make himself understood, won't he?
Julia:	Oh yes, he will, but it won't be easy for him. By the way, will we be allowed to use your computer to send emails?
Katie:	Yes, you will if there are not too many.

Übung 2 (Seite 21)

„Du bist nicht sehr gut in Englisch," sagt sein Vater. „Du hast noch nie gute Noten erzielen können (have never been able to). Und erinnerst du dich, wie du auf Malta nur wenig auf Englisch sagen konntest (could)?" „Das lag daran, dass ihr so gut Englisch sprechen könnt (can)", erwidert Stefan. „Ich hatte keine Möglichkeit." „Na ja, jetzt könnte (could) diese Reise dir eine gute Gelegenheit bieten", antwortet Julia. „Mandy und Mark, die in deinem Alter sind, werden dir alles zeigen können (will be able to), und du kannst (can) nur Englisch mit ihnen sprechen, weil sie kein Deutsch können (cannot speak)." Stefan scheint sich mit der Idee anzufreunden. „Aber werden Mark und ich ohne Mandy Sport treiben können (will be able to)? Ich könnte es nicht (couldn't) aushalten, mit einem Mädchen Fußball spielen zu müssen." „Wenn das dein einziges Problem ist", sagt sein Vater, „können (can) wir den Aufenthalt in England jetzt fest einplanen."

2.2 Modale Hilfsverben *may/might/must/to be allowed to*

Übung 1 (Seite 22)

1. What do I say if I want to have an egg for breakfast? May I have an egg for breakfast?
2. What do I say if I want to watch a football match on TV? May I watch the football on TV?
3. What do I say if I want to phone my parents? May I phone my parents?
4. What do I say if I want to borrow Mark's bike? May I borrow your bike, Mark?
5. What do I say if I want to use the Johnsons' internet? May I use the internet?

Übung 2 (Seite 23)

Do not pitch tents near the river. We were not allowed to pitch our tents near the river.
No ball games close to the tents. We were not allowed to play ball games close to the tents.
Do not use water from the river for cooking. We were not allowed to use water from the river for cooking.
Take fresh water only from the well. We were allowed to take fresh water only from the well.
Food may be cooked only outside the tents. We were allowed to cook only outside the tents.
No loud music after 10 pm. We were not allowed to play loud music after 10 pm.

2.3 Modale Hilfsverben *must/needn't/to have (got) to*

Übung 1 (Seite 25)

1. Du musst versuchen, immer freundlich zu sein. must
2. Du brauchst uns nicht jeden Tag anzurufen, aber du musst uns eine E-Mail schreiben. needn't/must
3. Du musst dich bedanken, wenn die Johnsons mit dir einen Ausflug machen. must
4. Du brauchst nicht die ganze Zeit zu reden, aber du musst auf Fragen antworten. needn't/must

Übung 2 (Seite 25)

1. I must go home now. I am so tired.
2. Mark's team has a football match on Saturday morning. He has to get up at 7 am.
3. It is 7.45 am and Mark has overslept. Now he must/has to hurry to be in time for the match.
4. On the way he meets Ben, who is also late. "We must run as fast as we can or we will miss the match," Ben says.
5. Katie wants to go riding with Anne this weekend, but she cannot go with her. Anne says, "I have to visit my grandparents in Dover, it is grandmother's birthday."
6. Stefan's teacher said to him, "You must work much harder if you want to get better grades in English."

2.4 Modales Hilfsverb *shall/should*

Übung 1 (Seite 26)

1. When Julia and Stefan come, I can bake a cake. Shall I bake a cake?
2. We can invite some friends. Shall we invite some friends?
3. I can put a 'welcome' sign on the front door. Shall I put a 'welcome' sign on the front door?
4. We could have a party. Shall we have a party?

Übung 2 (Seite 26)

1. Stefan doesn't work very hard in his English lessons. He should work harder.
2. Julia likes to tell Stefan what to do. She shouldn't be so bossy.
3. Mark's room is very untidy. He should put his things in the right place.
4. Mrs Grüner is worried about Stefan's visit to Britain. She shouldn't worry about it; everything will be fine.
5. It's better to tell the truth. You should always tell the truth.
6. Mandy is playing the recorder in the school concert, but she hasn't practised much yet. She should practise more often.

Übung 3 (Seite 27)

1. The twins watch too much television. They shouldn't watch so much television.
2. My football boots are dirty. I should clean them.
3. Mrs Johnson has put on weight. She should do more sport.
4. Mrs Johnson: I am overweight. I shouldn't go to work by car, I should walk.
5. Mandy to Mark: We have been late for school every day this week. We should leave home earlier.
6. Mr Johnson's car uses too much petrol. He should buy a more economical one.
7. Katie looks ill this morning. She shouldn't go to school.
8. It's very cold today. You should wear a scarf for cycling.

Abschlusstest

Aufgabe 1 (Seite 28)

1. Stefan may/might find it difficult to speak English.
2. He may not/might not always understand what you say.

3. You mustn't speak too quickly.
4. If he makes a mistake, you mustn't laugh.
5. Mum may/might give him some extra lessons in English.
6. And remember; Mandy, he may not/might not want to play football with you.

Aufgabe 2 (Seite 28)

1. "Will Stefan have to take his German-English dictionary to England?" "No, he won't, Katie has one he can use."
2. "Do pupils have to learn all the English irregular verbs?" "No, they don't, but their English would certainly improve if they did."
3. "Must we really/Do we really have to go to bed now?," the twins ask their mother. "Yes, you must/do, you both look very tired."
4. "Did Anne have to visit her grandparents recently?" "Yes, she did. It was her grandmother's birthday."
5. "Does Katie have to brush her horse every time she has ridden him?" "No, she doesn't. She does it because she likes it."
6. "Do you have to make such a mess in your bedroom?," Mrs Johnson asks Mark. "No, I don't, but I like it that way."

Aufgabe 3 (Seite 29)

Julia: I must go to Portobello Road when we visit London.
Katie: Why do you want to go there?
Julia: I saw the film 'Notting Hill' recently and many of the scenes show the market in Portobello Road. It must be very exciting to actually be there.
Katie: But we really needn't bother to go; nobody ever finds anything worth buying. Grandma Booth says that you have to be very careful that you don't buy something worth nothing at all.
Julia: But I don't have to buy anything. I just want to enjoy the atmosphere.
Katie: Well, alright, if you really want to.
Julia: There is one thing I must buy though. I just must have the video of the film in English.
Katie: You needn't buy it; we have a copy at home that you can borrow.

Aufgabe 4 (Seite 30)

1. You must be thirsty. Shall I get you something to drink?
2. It is very hot in here. Shall I open the window?
3. Are you hungry? Shall we get supper ready?
4. You both look very tired. Shall I show you to your rooms?
5. It's a lovely evening. Shall we play a game of tennis?
6. The sea looks beautiful. Shall we go for a swim?

Aufgabe 5 (Seite 30)

1. It's a fine day. Shall we have a picnic?
2. Mr Johnson's bike is covered in mud. He should clean it.
3. We could sing some songs at the party. Shall I bring my guitar?
4. Ben shouldn't be in goal again; he let in 5 goals in the last match.
5. Julia loves horses; Katie should let her brush Little Richard.
6. Stefan, you look bored. Shall we play a game of chess?

3.1 *Reflexive Pronouns*

Alles klar?! (Seite 32)

myself	ourselves
yourself	yourselves
himself	themselves
herself	
itself	

Es gibt auch noch eine unpersönliche Form: oneseIf

Help yourself/yourselves.	Bedient euch.
Enjoy yourself/yourselves.	Viel Spaß!
I did it all by myself.	Ich habe das alles allein gemacht.

Übung 1 (Seite 33)

1. Stefan has been sick on the ferry, he is feeling very sorry for himself.
2. When they arrive in Dover, Julia and Stefan carry their bags themselves.
3. When they meet the Johnsons, they introduce themselves.
4. Katie has looked after Stefan on the journey and is proud of herself.
5. As he was getting off the ferry Stefan fell down and hurt himself.
6. Katie is sure she will enjoy herself in England.
7. A cat can get down from a tree itself.
8. „We were very proud of ourselves at the end of the journey," Katie wrote to her mother.

Übung 2 (Seite 33)

Welcome to Canterbury, Julia and Stefan, we are very pleased to see you. We always have tea at this time, so please help yourselves. Mark and Mandy helped me to make the sandwiches before we left for Dover and Mark was a little clumsy and cut himself with a knife. The cake is a typically English fruit cake, I made it myself. We often ask ourselves what sort of meals you have in Germany and hope you like the English food. We hope to visit Germany one day ourselves and then we will learn what it is like. Anyway, now you are here and we hope you will enjoy yourselves.

Übung 3 (Seite 34)

1. sat down
2. were proud of themselves
3. baked … herself
4. were pleased
5. had to concentrate
6. will meet

Übung 4 (Seite 34)

1. The door to Julia's room opened and Katie came in with a cup of tea.
2. She told Julia to change so they could go and explore the town.
3. She said, they would meet her friend Mary in a café and enjoy themselves.
4. „Don't be afraid, she is very friendly," she said.
5. „I can remember the cathedral," said Julia, „I have seen it before."
6. When they get home they will help themselves to some tea and cake.

3.2 *Reciprocal Pronouns*

Übung 1 (Seite 35)

1. Katie and Anne live near each other.
2. When they go riding together they always enjoy themselves.
3. Stefan and Mark have not met before, they do not know each other.
4. Anne, don't brush Little Richard, I'd like to do it myself.
5. When it is the twins' birthday, they always give each other presents.
6. Julia and Katie are penfriends, they often write to each other/one another.

Übung 2 (Seite 35)

1. Now that the Booths are older, they often talk to themselves.
2. Mr and Mrs Booth were ill, so they had to look after each other.
3. Mark and Ben can look after themselves, they are good at judo.
4. Katie and Mary like riding together; it gives them time to talk to each other.
5. The twins do not need help from Katie, they can help each other.
6. Please, help yourselves, I hope you enjoy the meal.

3.3 *Prop Word one/ones*

Übung 1 (Seite 36)

1. "Katie, please lend me your pen to write my postcard." "Sorry Julia, I haven't got one."
2. Which sunglasses shall we buy for Dad, the black ones or the brown ones.
3. The twins have a cat, it is a black one.
4. Let's buy these shoes, Katie, they look smarter than the blue ones.
5. England has many cathedrals but Canterbury is a very famous one.
6. Which postcard shall I send Uncle Alan in Boston, this one or that one?

Übung 2 (Seite 36)

1. Katie, which would you like to ride: the black horse or the brown one?
2. Would you like this card or that one? Both, please.
3. Katie's horse is fast, but Anne's horse is the faster one.
4. Mark was the first of the twins to be born.
5. Mark's friend Ben has three sisters. Each one is pretty.
6. Canterbury and Dover are both popular tourist resorts but Dover is the one nearer the sea.

Abschlusstest

Aufgabe 1 (Seite 37)

1. Julia and Katie enjoyed themselves very much in town.
2. Sit down and help yourself.
3. I baked the cake myself.
4. The ferry will arrive on time, we are not afraid.

Aufgabe 2 (Seite 37)

1. Be careful of the candle, you might burn yourself.
2. Mary did not have riding lessons, she taught herself to ride.
3. Katie and Julia met in town to visit the cathedral.
4. They have been writing to each other for two years.
5. Katie fell off Little Richard and broke her arm.
6. She must concentrate better or she will fall off again.

Aufgabe 3 (Seite 37)

1. In the summer holidays Katie and Mary don't see each other very often.
2. Mandy and I give each other presents on our birthday.
3. My mother always bakes the cakes herself.
4. Mrs Johnson and her brother Alan were talking to each other on the phone.
5. Ben loves judo, he can't imagine himself doing any other sport.

Aufgabe 4 (Seite 38)

1. There is a tall tree in the garden and a short one.
2. Mark and Mandy always understand each other without speaking.
3. They seldom see themselves in the mirror.
4. There is a pink flower and a blue one in the vase.
5. The Johnsons' cat cleans itself every day.
6. Ben usually enjoys himself at judo club.

Aufgabe 5 (Seite 38)

1. Which desk is yours – the small one or the big one?
2. Which pen do you use – the blue one or the red one?
3. Which lesson do you prefer – the French one or the German one?
4. Which book are you reading – the old one or the new one?
5. Which lunch break shall we take – the first one or the second one?
6. Which schoolbag is yours – the leather one or the canvas one?

4.1 Unterscheidung Aktiv/Passiv

Übung 1 (Seite 41)

1. The Johnsons met Julia and Stefan at Dover.
2. The whole family gave them a warm welcome.
3. Mrs Johnson served Stefan and Julia a typical English breakfast.
4. Katie told Julia about Canterbury's history.
5. In the evening Katie and Mrs Johnson cooked a huge meal.
6. Mark found a dead mouse, which Maggie had caught.
7. Visitors buy thousands of postcards every year.
8. The twins will show Stefan round Canterbury.

4.2 Das Passiv in verschiedenen Zeiten

Alles klar?! (Seite 42)

Simple present – passive:

Guides	*tell*	*interesting facts*	*about the Cathedral.*
Interesting facts	are told		*about the Cathedral.*

Simple past – passive:

Murders	*killed*	*Thomas Beckett*	*in the Cathedral.*
Thomas Beckett	was killed		*in the Cathedral.*

Present perfect – passive:

More visitors than ever	*have visited*	*the Cathedral*	*this year.*
The Cathedral	has been visited	*by more visitors than ever*	*this year.*

Future – passive:

Visitors	*will learn*	*a lot*	*in a guided tour.*
A lot	will be learned / learnt		*in a guided tour.*

Und dann noch mit modalem Hilfsverb:

They	*can see*	*a lot of colourful windows*	*in the Cathedral.*
A lot of colourful windows	can be seen		*in the Cathedral.*

Übung 1 (Seite 43)

1. The Cathedral was rebuilt in the 11th century.
2. Julia and Stefan were taken to the Cathedral.
3. Stefan was told about the murder.
4. Many books have been written about the murder.
5. Photographs can be taken of the beautiful windows.
6. The monastery was closed in 1540.
7. Every year concerts are held in the Cathedral.
8. The twins will be woken at 7 am.
9. Stefan has been warned about the traffic on the left.
10. The new word cannot be found in the dictionary.

Übung 2 (Seite 44)

1. The Cathedral is visited by thousands of tourists every week.
2. A great number of photographs are always taken by the visitors.
3. Many beautiful windows were smashed by soldiers in the 17th century.
4. The windows were repaired by craftsmen.
5. Mark will be driven by Mr Johnson to the football match next Saturday.
6. A lot of cakes have just been made by Mrs Johnson.
7. Little Richard is ridden by Katie every week.
8. Some very beautiful songs were sung by the choir at the concert yesterday.

4.3 Besondere Formen

Übung 1 (Seite 45)

1. A number of houses were broken into by a burglar.
2. Stefan is often read to in English by Mrs Johnson.
3. Stefan's language problems were talked about by Mr and Mrs Johnson.
4. The photos of Canterbury Cathedral were looked at by Stefan's parents.
5. The clown's tricks were laughed at by the audience.
6. Maggie will be looked after by Anne when the Johnsons are away.

Übung 2 (Seite 46)

1. A lot of new ideas were thought of at the meeting yesterday.
2. Mark's school bag is looked for by all the family every morning.
3. Mark's parents were spoken to by the teacher last week.
4. Maggie has been fed and played with by the twins twice today.
5. Mark and Mandy's old toys must be thrown away by Mrs Johnson.
6. The entrance fees will be paid for by Mr Johnson.

Lerntipp (Seite 47)

They offered me a guided tour.
They offered you a guided tour.
They offered him a guided tour.
They offered her a guided tour.
They offered us a guided tour.
They offered you a guided tour.
They offered them a guided tour.

I was offered a guided tour.
You were offered a guided tour.
He was offered a guided tour.
She was offered a guided tour.
We were offered a guided tour.
You were offered a guided tour.
They were offered a guided tour.

Übung 3 (Seite 48)

1. All visitors are offered a warm welcome.
2. Visitors are shown the Cathedral.
3. The first Archbishop was given a church in Canterbury.
4. Stefan was told the story of Thomas Beckett's murder.
5. Jan was sent some pictures of the Cathedral.
6. Stefan was promised a visit to the Edinburgh Tattoo.

Übung 4 (Seite 48)

1. The old houses must be pulled down.
2. The Cathedral guide book can be bought in the souvenir shop.
3. The tourists were shown the town.
4. The school has been promised ten new computers.
5. The visitors were told some interesting facts.
6. Maps of Canterbury are sold in every big shop.

Übung 5 (Seite 49)

1. Julia was lent an umbrella.
2. Mark has been promised a new bicycle.
3. Julia was sold a guidebook.
4. Julia and Stefan were shown the beautiful coastline.
5. The choir was taught a new song.
6. Mark was paid five pounds to cut the grass.

Übung 6 (Seite 49)

1. She was asked a question.
2. He was lent a dictionary.
3. He was promised a new computer.
4. They were sent an email.
5. Will we be told some interesting stories?
6. You will be given a fascinating tour of the town.

Übung 7 (Seite 50)

It is known that Thomas Beckett was killed in the Cathedral. It is reported that four knights were the murderers. It is said that the king and Thomas Beckett were once good friends. It is believed that Thomas Beckett became more loyal to the Pope than to the king once he was made Archbishop of Canterbury. It is thought that the king was angry with Thomas Beckett for many different reasons. It is understood that the four knights really thought that the king wanted Thomas Beckett to die. It is reported that the king later went on a pilgrimage to Canterbury, barefoot and in sackcloth, to show his sorrow.

Abschlusstest

Aufgabe 1 (Seite 51)

1. Tennis is sometimes played at the twin's school.
2. More vegetables than fruit are grown in the Johnsons' garden.
3. What kind of cake is sold at the shop?
4. Do you know where the tennis balls are kept?
5. How often is rubbish collected in Canterbury?
6. Why is Mrs Grüner worried about Stefan's visit to England?

Aufgabe 2 (Seite 51)

1. Thousands of postcards have been bought by the visitors.
2. Tea and cakes are served in the Cathedral restaurant by volunteers.
3. Julia and Stefan were taken to the funfair by the Johnsons.
4. The visitors will be shown where Thomas Beckett died by guides.
5. The grass is cut by Mr Johnson every week.
6. Mrs Johnson's favourite necklace has been broken by Katie.

Aufgabe 3 (Seite 52)

All mobile phones must be switched off immediately.
Library books cannot be given back on Saturdays.
Mark's room must be tidied up soon.
Most of the football matches have been fixed up for the next season.
The old oak tree was cut down last week.
The plates and dishes have been cleared away after the party.

Aufgabe 4 (Seite 52)

1. It is known that elephants can get very old.
2. Little Richard is brushed every day.
3. I hope that your room will soon be tidied up.
4. The shop has been closed.
5. It is understood that the teachers won't strike.
6. The visitors were shown a film./A film was shown to the visitors.
7. Three languages are taught in the new school.
8. Many jokes were told at the party.
9. I was lent 10 Euros/10 Euros were lent to me.
10. The strange insect was looked at for a long time.

5.1 *Direct Speech/Reported Speech*

Übung 1 (Seite 54)

qutewndto answerforeto sayvkfed to reportkwüdto tellmref to remarkburlfto replymwptfsdv to agreekbmeofto explainlhnrto thinknmeigej

Übung 2 (Seite 55)

1. Mr and Mrs Johnson explain that they will all go to London tomorrow.
2. Katie tells Julia that they will go shopping in Oxford Street.
3. The twins explain that they are going to Madame Tussaud's.
4. Stefan says that he wants to see the London Eye.
5. Julia informs Stefan that she can't go with him because she is going with Katie.

Übung 3 (Seite 56)

1. "Mandy, Grandma Booth called, she can't get tickets for you for Madame Tussaud's."
2 "Katie, Anne called. Can you ring her back, she wants to tell you something about Little Richard."
3 "I called the station. They said if we want to be in London before 10, we must catch the train at 8 am."
4 "Mark, Ben called. He can't go with you to judo class this evening."
5 "Dad called. He missed his train, he won't be home in time to have supper with us."

Übung 4 (Seite 56)

1. Katie tells her mother that she and Julia are going to go shopping in London.
   Katie to her mother: Mum, Julia and I are going to go shopping in London.
2. Julia says she has left her map of London at home.
   Julia: I have left my map of London at home.
3. Mr Johnson doesn't think that the girls should go shopping alone.
   Mr Johnson to the girls: I don't think you should go shopping alone.
4. Mrs Johnson told Mark that he and Mandy can't go to Madame Tussaud's on their own.
   Mrs Johnson: Mark, you and Mandy can't go to Madame Tussaud's on your own.

5.2 *Backshift of Tenses*

Übung 1 (Seite 58)

1. Julia said that she liked London very much, there was so much to see.
2. Stefan said yes, they were having a wonderful time.
3. Julia said she loved shopping in Oxford St., she had never seen so many interesting shops and people from all over the world.
4. Stefan said he was sure Julia had spent all her holiday money.
5. Julia said no, she hadn't! They were going to the London Eye the next day and she needed some money for postcards.
6. Stefan said he had posted all his cards to his friends and he had written them all in English.
7. Julia said they really had to go and buy an umbrella as it was going to rain.
8. Stefan said they would phone again soon; they were going to have so much to tell them when they got home, it would take them hours!

5.3 *Reported Speech with Auxiliary Verbs*

Übung 1 (Seite 59)

1. Mrs Johnson said that they had to take the train at eight o'clock.
   We must take the train at eight o'clock.
2. Mrs Johnson said they might take a boat on the Thames to Hampton Court.
   We may take a boat on the Thames to Hampton Court.
3. Mrs Johnson said they couldn't go to Madame Tussaud's but they were able to go to the London Eye.
   We can't go to Madame Tussaud's but we can go to the London Eye.
4. Mrs Johnson said they had to take an umbrella in case it rained.
   We must take an umbrella in case it rains.

5.4 *Questions*

Übung 1 (Seite 60)

1. Julia asked where they could go shopping.
2. Stefan asked when they could go to the London Eye.
3. Julia asked if they could see a musical in the West End.
4. The Johnsons asked whether they wanted to see the Millennium Bridge.

5.5 *Commands and Requests*

Übung 1 (Seite 61)

1. Can you meet me at six o'clock?
2. Can you take us to the London Eye?
3. Can you tell me the history of Hampton Court?
4. Be quiet, please!

5.6 *Adverbials of Place and Time*

Übung 1 (Seite 62)

1. The twins said they couldn't go to the Millennium Bridge that day. (today)
2. They told Julia they had been there the day before. (yesterday)
3. Katie said she would go shopping with Julia in Oxford St. the next day. (tomorrow)
4. She said they would see many tourists there. (here)
5. Julia said she and Stefan had arrived in Canterbury two weeks before. (two weeks ago)
6. Mr Johnson said they would return to Canterbury the following week. (next week)

Abschlusstest

Aufgabe 1 (Seite 63)

1. Julia: Stefan and I have been in England for two weeks.
   Julia said that Stefan and she had been in England for two weeks.
2. Stefan: I am not very good at English yet.
   Stefan said that he was not very good at English yet.
3. Mandy: I don't really like shopping in big cities.
   Mandy has just told me that she doesn't really like shopping in big cities.
4. Mark: Can I go to London Zoo?
   Mark has just asked if he can go to London Zoo.
5. Stefan: When can we go to the Hard Rock Café?
   Stefan asked when they could go to the Hard Rock Café.
6. Katie: I hope we will be able to come to London again.
   Katie said she hoped they would be able to come to London again.
7. Mrs Johnson: Hurry up, please, we'll miss the train.
   Mrs Johnson told them to hurry up, they would miss the train.

Aufgabe 2 (Seite 63)

1. Stefan said he hoped he would be able to see the London Eye.
   I hope I will be able to see the London Eye.
2. Mark said he did not know where the Millennium Bridge was.
   I do not know where the Millennium Bridge is.
3. Julia said Stefan had been seasick on the ferry two weeks before.
   Stefan was seasick on the ferry two weeks ago.
4. The twins said they had not been able to go to Madame Tussaud's the day before.
   We were not able to go to Madame Tussaud's yesterday.
5. Mr Johnson said the train had been late again.
   The train was late again.

Aufgabe 3 (Seite 64)

1. Katie's parents told her that she could not go shopping alone.
2. The twins said they wanted to see the London Eye.
3. Julia wrote to her mother that she had seen "Cats" in London.
4. Stefan wrote to his mother that he did not like English food.
5. Julia said that Stefan was now better at English.
6. Mrs Johnson told her husband that the time in London had been lovely.

Aufgabe 4 (Seite 64)

1. Mark asked when they could go to Madame Tussaud's.
   When can we go to Madame Tussaud's?
2. Mandy asked if she could go shopping with Katie and Julia.
   Can I go shopping with Katie and Julia?
3. Mrs Johnson asked whether they wanted to see a musical.
   Do you want to see a musical?
4. Katie asked when they could go to the theatre.
   When can we go to the theatre?
5. Stefan asked whether he might go to the London Eye.
   May I go to the London Eye?
6. Mr Johnson asked when they had to return to Canterbury.
   When must we/do we have to return to Canterbury?

6.1 *Conditional Clauses (If-Clauses)*

Übung 1 (Seite 67)

1. If the Johnsons are lucky, they will get tickets for the Tattoo.
2. If the young people go to the Tattoo, Mr and Mrs Johnson will go to a concert.
3. Stefan won't be pleased, if the bands don't play the bagpipes.
4. If Katie and Julia go shopping, the twins will book a tour of Edinburgh.
5. If Stefan takes some photographs of Edinburgh, he will be able to show them to Jan.
6. Katie will get a headache, if the drummers do not stop playing soon.

Übung 2 (Seite 67)

1. If they went to Holyrood House, they would learn about Mary Stuart.
2. If they read Schiller's play 'Maria Stuart', they would know about her fate.
3. If he were a Scot, Stefan would love to play the bagpipes.
4. Katie would enjoy the Scottish breakfast if she liked porridge.
5. If the Johnsons hired a car, they would be able to tour the Highlands.
6. They would be able to see the monster if they went to Loch Ness.

Übung 3 (Seite 68)

1. If Stefan and Mark visit Glasgow, they will see a Celtic football match.
2. Her friends at home would laugh if Julia bought a kilt.
3. Mr Johnson would go salmon fishing if he had enough time.
4. If Katie and Julia get up early tomorrow, they will go shopping in Princes Street.
5. If Mr Johnson goes to St Andrew's, he will play a game of golf.
6. If he takes a photograph of Nessie, Stefan will send it to a newspaper.
7. If Mrs Johnson liked biscuits, she would buy a tin of shortbread.
8. If Katie could drive, she would visit Balmoral.

6.2 *Adverbial Clauses*

Übung 1 (Seite 70)

1. They stayed in their hotel until it was time for the Tattoo.
2. They met for the Tattoo after they had been shopping.
3. They queued in the interval so that they could buy a drink.
4. Julia and Stefan could not join in when the audience sang „Scotland the Brave".
5. They didn't sing „Scotland the Brave" because they didn't know the words.
6. Although they were tired, they went to a disco after the Tattoo.

Übung 2 (Seite 70)

1. Since I've been in Scotland, I've seen a lot of interesting sights.
2. We visited the Castle and stayed until it closed.
3. We are leaving Edinburgh tomorrow so that we can visit the Lake District on the way home.
4. We might stop in Grasmere where the Johnsons' relatives live.
5. I would like to visit the Lake District because I am fond of walking.
6. It will be fun to walk on the fells although I haven't got my walking boots with me.

6.3 *Relative Clauses*

Übung 1 (Seite 72)

1. The recorder which/that Mandy has played for five years needs to be repaired.
2. The teacher who/that taught my mother French is now teaching me.
3. The hotel which/that the Johnsons had booked was near the Castle.
4. The music which/that Stefan heard at the Tattoo was very loud.
5. The horse which/that you saw yesterday was Little Richard.
6. The Lake District is one of the places in England which/that tourists like to visit.

Übung 2 (Seite 72)

1. The recorder Mandy has played for five years needs to be repaired.
2. kein *contact clause*
3. The hotel the Johnsons had booked was near the Castle.
4. The music Stefan heard at the Tattoo was very loud.
5. The horse you saw yesterday was Little Richard.
6. The Lake District is one of the places in England tourists like to visit.

Übung 3 (Seite 72)

1. The man whom Stefan spoke to was a Scot.
2. The guide whose uniform was blue talked to Stefan.
3. The band whose members wore kilts played the bagpipes.
4. The part of England (which/that) they wanted to go to was the Lake District.
5. The man whom they saw in front of the band was the conductor.
6. The kilt (which/that) Katie was looking at in the shop window was very expensive.

Übung 4 (Seite 73)

1. Mr Johnson, who is keen to protect the environment, usually cycles to work.
2. Mark's football team, which is one of the best in the school league, has just won the cup.
3. Stefan, whose grades in English have never been good, now finds English fun.
4. Mandy, to whom Mark is sometimes quite rude, can be very bossy.
5. Edinburgh Castle, which the Johnsons enjoyed visiting, is at the top of a steep hill.
6. The monster, which is said to live in Loch Ness, has hardly ever been seen.

Übung 5 (Seite 73)

1. Many people who go to the Lake District want to walk on the fells.
2. The school choir, which gives two concerts a year, has learned three new songs.
3. Katie, who loves riding, is not sure whether she can afford any more lessons.
4. Mark, who is very untidy, has lost his football boots.
5. The boy who is brushing Little Richard is Anne's brother.
6. The dress which Julia is wearing was made by her mother.

6.4 *Infinitives*

Übung 1 (Seite 74)

1. Julia asked Mrs Johnson to help her.
2. Julia finds it easier to speak English.
3. It is sometimes difficult for Katie to understand German.
4. His father taught Mark to swim.
5. It is wrong to walk in the Lake District without walking boots.
6. Their parents allowed the twins to go to the disco after the Tattoo.

Abschlusstest

Aufgabe 1 (Seite 75)

1. If Stefan worked harder, he would get better grades.
2. If Katie has more lessons, she will be a better rider/If Katie had more lessons, she would be a better rider.
3. They will see lakes and mountains if they go to the Highlands./They would see lakes and mountains if they went to the Highlands.
4. If they walked on the fells, they would be fit.
5. If it rains at the Tattoo tomorrow, they will get wet.
6. Mr Johnson would move to the Lake District if he could retire.

Aufgabe 2 (Seite 75)

1. After they had been to the disco, they went back to the hotel.
2. They left Edinburgh in the evening so that they could spend a whole day in the Lake District.
3. They wanted to go the Lake District because the Johnsons had relatives there.
4. While the young people were at the Tattoo, Mr and Mrs Johnson went to a concert.
5. They didn't go to the Tattoo because it was too loud for them.
6. They visited Holyrood House where they learnt a lot about Mary Stuart's life.

Aufgabe 3 (Seite 75/76)

1. When Mr Johnson cycles to work, he always puts on a helmet.
2. Although Stefan did not like the English breakfast at first, he now enjoys it.
3. They are having a drink in the bar until it is time for the concert.
4. The twins try to speak very clearly so that Stefan can understand them.
5. We had to hurry to the Castle as it closed at 6 pm.
6. Stefan wrote all his postcards while he was in the Lake District.

Aufgabe 4 (Seite 76)

1. That's the boy whom Mark sits next to at school.
2. This is the cousin whose family lives in the Lake District.
3. That is the horse on which Katie rides/which Katie rides on.
4. This is the programme about horses to which Katie listens every day/which Katie listens to every day.
5. That is the guide whom Stefan spoke to/to whom Stefan spoke.
6. That is the waitress whom Mr Johnson gave the large tip to/to whom Mr Johnson gave the large tip.

7.1. *Understanding a Text*

Übung 1 (Seite 80)

Lösungsvorschlag:

a) The text is written as a report. However, stories are included which often seem closer to fiction than fact.

b) The subject of the text is how the legend of the Loch Ness monster developed.

Übung 2 (Seite 80)

Lösungsvorschlag:

a) Who? – George Spicer and his wife; What? –"an extraordinary form of animal" about one metre high and eight metres long; Where? – on the new road alongside Loch Ness; When? 1933; How? – the animal crawled across the road, leaving a trail of broken branches behind it.

b) It is, on the one hand, hard to believe that George Spicer and his wife made everything up (erfinden) as they described the animal in great detail. On the other hand, it is difficult to imagine that scientists could not prove the existence of so large a creature with such an unusual neck. It seems more likely that the story is not true.

c) Stefan is really fascinated by the story of Nessie. He is so keen to take a photo of the monster and become rich and famous as a result that he will no doubt return to Scotland one day to make this dream come true.

Übung 3 (Seite 81)

a) Loch Ness is situated in the Highlands 37 km southwest of Inverness.

b) Nessie became the cause of interest because a new road was built in 1933 alongside the remote lake.

c) The first sighting happened shortly after the road was built.

d) He claimed he had nearly hit the creature on a moonlit night.

e) A trick photograph of Nessie was published to annoy the paper, which had made fun of one of its writers in an article.

f) There have been a number of searches with sonar equipment and underwater cameras.

g) They have been explained as a misidentification of known animals, a tree trunk, a trick or even a paranormal experience.

h) Some people are not convinced of Nessie's existence because no physical evidence has been found.

Übung 4 (Seite 81)

to cross; to follow; to crawl; to swim;to get off
to go; to jump; to run: to hop; to walk; etc ...

Übung 5 (Seite 81)

life	to live	attempt	to attempt
building	to build	explanation	to explain
description	to describe	remains	to remain
proof	to prove		
suggestion	to suggest		

Übung 6 (Seite 82)

#

(Die folgenden Textergänzungen stellen nur eine von vielen Ergänzungsmöglichkeiten dar.)
From Edinburgh to the Highlands and back was a long way, the journey would take too long. Mr and Mrs Johnson also wanted to visit their relatives who live in the Lake District.They had not seen them for a very long time. The twins wanted to go walking on the fells. Stefan was disappointed because the story of Nessie had captured his imagination and he had hoped they would arrive in time to catch sight of Nessie on one of her rare appearances and he had also hoped to take a photo of her and send it to a newspaper to make him rich and famous. He decided that he would return some time in the future to Scotland to search for Nessie for himself and see whether she really existed. He is quite certain that he will be the only person to prove that there really is a monster in the lake.

Abschlusstest

Aufgabe 1 (Seite 83)

1. shallow	deep
2. first	last
3. in front of	behind
4. narrow	wide
5. thick	thin
6. upper	lower
7. unknown	known
8. finally	initially

Aufgabe 2 (Seite 83)

1. to become the cause of interest	interessant werden
2. the width of the road	die Breite der Straße
3. remote	entlegen
4. the trail of broken branches	die Spur von abgebrochenen Ästen
5. traces of movement in the water	Zeichen von Bewegung im Wasser
6. the first sighting of Nessie	das erste Mal, als Nessie gesehen wurde
7. turned out to be a trick	erwies sich als Trick
8. the aim was to annoy	die Absicht war, ... zu ärgern
9. an inanimate object	ein lebloser Gegenstand
10. it is worth noting	es ist erwähnenswert

Aufgabe 3 (Seite 84)

1. shallow	water
2. fictitious	story
3. frightening	experience
4. lively	discussion
5. convincing	proof
6. successful	attempt

8.1 Den Wortschatz sichern und erweitern

Übung 1 (Seite 87)

Odd man out

- to see, ~~to listen~~, to taste, to smell, to feel
- to walk, to run, to crawl, ~~to sit~~
- to cycle, ~~to run~~, to drive, to go by train
- second, minute, hour, day, ~~clock~~

Übung 2 (Seite 88)

- **bei Adjektiven**

clean – dirty
difficult – easy
happy – unhealthy
healthy – unhealthy
high – low
poor – rich
possible – impossible
slow – fast

- **bei Nomen**

day – night
morning – evening
spring – autumn
summer – winter

- **bei Verben**

to arrive – to leave
to finish – to begin
to hate – to love
to hurry up – to slow down
to laugh – to cry
to start – to stop

- **bei Adverbien**

always – never
indoors – outdoors
late – early
sometimes – often

Übung 3 (Seite 88)

to go	by bus
to go to	London
to plan	a trip
to practise	English
to visit	places

8.2 Arbeit mit dem Wörterbuch

Übung 1 (Seite 91)

a)

Informationen	**Wo stehen sie?**	**Wie heißen sie hier?**
Buchstabe im Alphabet	Seitenrand	C
blaues Leitwort	obere, äußere Seitenecke	child
blaues Stichwort	alphabetisch richtige Stelle	chip
Hochzahl	nach dem Stichwort	1

b) 1. angeschlagene Stelle (z. B. an Tasse, Teller, aber auch: an Vase, Becher, Waschbecken)
2. Splitter, Span (z. B. an einem Stück Holz, aber auch: an Porzellan, Glas, Schokolade)
3. Pommes frites – aber nur im britischen Englisch! (Pl. BE = Plural, British English)
4. (Kartoffel-)Chips – aber nur im amerikanischen Englisch! (Pl. AE = Plural, American English)
5. Spielmarke, Chip (z. B. beim Roulette, aber auch: beim Brettspiel, für Spielautomaten)
6. Chip (in der Elektrotechnik, z. B. Mikrochip beim Computer, Speicherchip der Digitalkamera)

c) When Tom was in London, he ate chips every day.
Als Tom in London war, hat er jeden Tag Pommes frites gegessen.

8.3 Situationen meistern

Übung 1 (Seite 93)

Shop assistant:	Good morning. Can I help you?
Julia:	Yes, please. I'm looking for a new T-shirt.
Shop assistant:	Let's see. We've got some nice ones over there. Have a look. Young people like them very much. How do you like them?
Julia:	Hmm, not so much really. I don't like the colours. This pink is really shocking. Could you show me something else? How about those over there? They look really cool.
Shop assistant:	Would you like to try one on? What's your size?
Julia:	I think small is fine. It looks great. ... How much is it?
Shop assistant:	It's £10.
Julia:	£10? Ok, I'll take it.

Übung 2 (Seite 94)

Shop assistant:	Good morning. Can I help you?
Katie:	Yes, please. I'm looking for a pair of sandals.
Shop assistant:	Let's see. We've got some nice ones over there. Have a look. How do you like them?
Katie:	Hmm, not so much really. The style is nice, but I wanted red ones. Have you got those in red?
Shop assistant:	No, I'm sorry. But how about those over there?
Katie:	Ahh ... they look really cool. And I like the colour very much.
Shop assistant:	Would you like to try one on? What's your size?
Katie:	I think size 6 is fine. But could you tell me first how much they are?
Shop assistant:	They are £35.
Katie:	£35! That's too expensive for me. I'll have to ask my mother first.
Shop assistant:	Well, I'm sorry, but we don't have any cheaper ones.
Katie:	Well, thank you. I think I'll have to look somewhere else then. Good bye.
Shop assistant:	Good bye.

Abschlusstest

Aufgabe 1 (Seite 95)

1. cheap – expensive
2. dark – pale
3. exciting – unexciting
4. friendly – unfriendly
5. big – small
6. long – short
7. successful – unsuccessful
8. usual – unusual

Aufgabe 2 (Seite 95)

1. Excuse me, could you please help me?
b) Du bittest um Hilfe.

2. I'm looking for an interesting, not so difficult book.
d) Du fragst nach einem interessanten, nicht so schwierigen Buch.

3. Could I please try these shoes on?
a) Du fragst, ob du die Schuhe anprobieren kannst.

4. They are too small. Have you got a bigger size?
c) Du sagst, dass die Schuhe zu klein sind, und fragst, ob sie ein größeres Paar haben.

5. I'm afraid this is too expensive for me. Do you have something cheaper?
e) Du sagst, dass etwas zu teuer für dich ist, und fragst, ob es etwas Billigeres gibt.

Aufgabe 3 (Seite 96)

1. Du sagst, dass du dich nur umschauen willst.
I'm just looking around.

2. Du bittest darum, dass man dir etwas anderes zeigt.
Could you show me something else?

3. Du fragst, wie viel das T-Shirt kostet.
How much is the T-shirt?

4. Du sagst, dass du es kaufst.
I'll take it.

5. Du bedankst dich und verabschiedest dich.
Thanks and good bye.

Irregular Verbs

Infinitiv	Past Simple	Past Participle	Deutsch
be	was/were	been	sein
beat	beat	beaten	schlagen
become	became	become	werden
bend	bent	bent	biegen
begin	began	begun	beginnen, anfangen
blow	blew	blown	blasen
break	broke	broken	brechen
bring	brought	brought	bringen
build	built	built	bauen
buy	bought	bought	kaufen
catch	caught	caught	fangen
choose	chose	chosen	wählen
come	came	come	kommen
cost	cost	cost	kosten
cut	cut	cut	schneiden
do	did	done	tun, machen
draw	drew	drawn	zeichnen
drink	drank	drunk	trinken
drive	drove	driven	fahren
eat	ate	eaten	essen
fall	fell	fallen	fallen
feed	fed	fed	füttern
feel	felt	felt	fühlen
fight	fought	fought	kämpfen
find	found	found	finden
fly	flew	flown	fliegen
forbid	forbade	forbidden	verbieten
forget	forgot	forgotten	vergessen
get	got	got	bekommen
give	gave	given	geben
go	went	gone	gehen
grow	grew	grown	wachsen
hang	hung	hung	(auf)hängen
have	had	had	haben
hear	heard	heard	hören

Infinitiv	Past Simple	Past Participle	Deutsch
hide	hid	hidden	verstecken
hit	hit	hit	schlagen, treffen
hold	held	held	halten
hurt	hurt	hurt	verletzen
keep	kept	kept	behalten
know	knew	known	kennen, wissen
lay	laid	laid	legen
lead	led	led	führen, leiten
leave	left	left	verlassen
lend	lent	lent	verleihen
let	let	let	lassen
lie	lay	lain	liegen
lose	lost	lost	verlieren
make	made	made	machen
mean	meant	meant	bedeuten
meet	met	met	treffen
pay	paid	paid	bezahlen
put	put	put	setzen, stellen, legen
read	read	read	lesen
ride	rode	ridden	reiten
ring	rang	rung	klingeln
rise	rose	risen	aufgehen
run	ran	run	rennen
say	said	said	sagen
see	saw	seen	sehen
sell	sold	sold	verkaufen
send	sent	sent	schicken
set	set	set	setzen, stellen
shake	shook	shaken	schütteln
shine	shone	shone	scheinen
shoot	shot	shot	schießen
show	showed	shown	zeigen
shut	shut	shut	schließen
sing	sang	sung	singen
sink	sank	sunk	sinken, untergehen
sit	sat	sat	sitzen
sleep	slept	slept	schlafen

Infinitiv	Past Simple	Past Participle	Deutsch
speak	spoke	spoken	sprechen
spend	spent	spent	ausgeben, verbringen
stand	stood	stood	stehen
steal	stole	stolen	stehlen
Strike	struck	struck	treffen
swim	swam	swum	schwimmen
swing	swung	swung	schwingen
take	took	taken	nehmen, dauern
teach	taught	taught	unterrichten
tear	tore	torn	zerreißen
tell	told	told	erzählen
think	thought	thought	denken
throw	threw	thrown	werfen
understand	understood	understood	verstehen
wake	woke	woken	aufwecken
wear	wore	worn	tragen (Kleidung)
win	won	won	gewinnen
write	wrote	written	schreiben

Bildnachweis
PantherMedia: Seite 8 © Anja Greiner Adam; Seite 68 © Thomas Pirtschke
PIXELIO: Seite 5 © Birgit
Shutterstock: Seite 19 © J.T. Lewis; Seite 41 und Seite 50 © Philip Lange; Seite 53 © David Clegg; Seite 61 © Benson HE; Seite 65 © Clint Clearley; Seite 79 © CJPhoto; Seite 97 © Jozsef Szasz-Fabian
www.fotolia.de: Seite 10 © Lianem; Seite 15 © ProfphotoXL; Seite 23 © Galyna Andrushko; Seite 25 © KeeT; Seite 31 © Ewe Degiampietro; Seite 32 © Bek; Seite 39 © Birgit Reitz-Hofmann; Seite 40 © TheThirdMan; Seite 44 (links) © Christopher Nolan; Seite 44 (rechts) © Mark Physsas; Seite 62 © mintcake668; Seite 77 © felixbruno; Seite 82 © chandelle; Seite 87 © Meddie Popcorn; Seite 92 © Peter Girling; Seite 93 © Tomasz Trojanowski; Seite 121 © Teamarbeit
Bilddatenbank Langenscheidt: Seite 27, 58, 85 und 89

Nachwort

Bäume können Lehrern, Therapeuten und allen, die sich weiterentwickeln oder schöpferische Lösungen für Probleme finden wollen, von großem Nutzen sein.

Ein „intelligenter" Kontakt mit unserer natürlichen Umwelt setzt voraus, daß wir durch unmittelbare Erfahrung lernen und eine Lehrzeit durchmachen. Dann können wir beispielsweise Kindern die Werkzeuge in die Hand geben, die sie brauchen, um eigenes Wissen zu erwerben und Talente zu nutzen, die in unserem Schulsystem oft brachliegen. Ein solcher Lernstil fördert die Freude am Entdecken und ermutigt den Lernenden, tiefer in die Materie einzudringen - denn was er entdeckt, ist lebendig. Auch Kinder können mit ihrer Lebenskraft Kontakt aufnehmen und begreifen, daß sie mit der ganzen Natur verbunden sind. Auf diese Weise lernen sie, das Leben zu achten - ihr eigenes Leben und das Leben anderer Menschen. Außerdem wird ihnen bewußt, daß die Wirklichkeit viele Facetten hat und daß sie die Ansichten anderer respektieren und ihr eigenes Urteilsvermögen verfeinern können, ohne zu verurteilen.

Es gibt viele Möglichkeiten, die von der Natur inspirierte Kreativität zu nutzen und zu genießen. Dieses Buch bietet Ihnen kein neues theoretisches System und keine Patentlösungen an, sondern Werkzeuge, die Ihnen helfen, neue Denkweisen und neue Einstellungen zu entwickeln.

Ich glaube, daß die Menschheit gerade im Begriff ist, eine neue Ebene der Wirklichkeit zu entdecken. Die Saat unseres Potentials beginnt in uns allen zu wachsen und wird, wenn sie blüht, die Welt grundlegend verändern. Ich hoffe, daß die schöpferische Begegnung mit den Wundern der Natur dieser Saat hilft, zu wachsen und zu gedeihen.

Quellen

Dictionnaire des symbols, Robert Lafont, Paris, 1969

Flore forestière Francaise, tome 1, Idf edition (Ministère de l'Agriculture Français), Paris, 1989

Brahma Kumaris, *Visions of a better world,* A United Nations Peace Messenger Publication, London, 1992

Bross, Jacques, *Les arbres de France,* Plon, 1987

Chase, Pamela Louise and Pawlik, Jonathan, *Trees for Healing,* Newcastle Publishing Co Inc, California, 1991

Coats, Callum, *Living Energies,* Gateway Books, Bath, 1996

Cook, Roger, *The Tree of Life,* Thames and Hudson, London, 1995

Gimbel, Theo, *Heilen mit Farbe,* AT, Aarau, 1994

Honervogt, Tanmaya, *Reiki,* Gaia Books Ltd, London, 1998

Langer, Ellen, *Fit im Kopf,* Rowohlt, Hamburg, 1996

McLean, Dorothy, *To Honor the Earth,* Harper, San Francisco, 1991

Mees, Dr L F C, *La maladie ... une bénédiction,* Les Trois Arches, Chatou, 1987

Mendelsohn, Robert, *Wie Ihr Kind gesund aufwachsen kann,* Mahajiva, Holzhausen, 1994

Milner, J Edward, *The Tree Book,* Collins and Brown, London, 1992

Mindell, Arnold, *Der Leib der Träume,* Junfermann, Paderborn, 1987

Paterson, Jacqueline Memory, *Tree Wisdom,* Thorsons, London, 1996

Pearce, Fred, *Die grünen Macher,* Rotbuch, Berlin, 1991

Popcorn, Faith and Marigold, Lys, *Clicking,* Heyne, München 1996

Pribram, *Synchronicity,* Bantam Books, 1987

Purce, Jill, *Die Spirale,* Kösel, München, 1993

Sheldrake, Rupert, *Sieben Experimente, die die Welt verändern,* Goldmann, München 1998

—*The Rebirth of Nature,* Bantam Books, 1991

Vogt, Nathalie and Michel, *La Foret du Rhin secrète et légendaire,* published by the authors, 1995

Fotonachweis

p 2, 6-7, 8-9, Alan Watson/Forest Light (FL); p 10-11 David Woodfall/Woodfall Wild Images (WWI); p 13, 14-5, 16 Alan Watson/FL; p 17 Maurizio Biancarelli/WWI; p 21 Ronald Sheridan/Ancient Art and Architecture; p 22-3 *background image:* Science Photo Library; p 22 Alan Watson/FL; p 23 *from top:* Alan Watson/FL, Gaia Books, Steve Austin/WWI, Biophoto Associates/SPL; p 26-7 Steve Teague; p 31 Rob Blakers/WWI; p 34-5, 36-7 Alan Watson/FL; p 38 Kathy Collins/WWI; p 39 David Woodfall/WWI; p 40-41 Deni Bown; p 47 John MacPherson/WWI; p 50, 52-3 Alan Watson/FL; p 57, 58 Gaia Books; p 59 Bob Gibbons/WWI; p 61 Gaia Books; p 62 Mark Hamblin/WWI; p 63, 64-5 Maurizio Biancarelli/WWI; p 67, 71 Alan Watson/FL; p 72-3 Kathy Collins/WWI; p 74 Nigel Hicks/WWI; p 77 Alan Watson/FL; p 80-1 David Woodfall/WWI; p 82-3, 86 Alan Watson/FL; p 88 Deni Bown; p 89 David Woodfall/WWI; p 93 Patrice Bouchardon; p 94 Kathy Collins/WWI; p 95 Niall Benvie/Oxford Scientific Films (OSF); p 96 Deni Bown; p 97 Steve Austin/WWI; p 98 Maurizio Biancarelli/WWI; p 99 Alan Watson/FL; p 100 Hans Reinhard/OSF; p 101 Niall Benvie/OSF; p 102 Deni Bown/OSF; p 103 David Woodfall/WWI; p 104, p 105 *top:* Bob Gibbons/WWI; *bottom:* Deni Bown/OSF; p 106 Niall Benvie/OSF; p 107 Alan Watson/FL; p 108 William Paton/OSF; p 109 Alan Watson/FL; p 110, 111 David Woodfall/WWI; p 112 Deni Bown; p 113 *top:* Steve Austin/WWI; *bottom:* John Robinson/WWI; p 114 Steve Austin/WWI; p 115 David Woodfall/WWI; p 116 Deni Bown; p 118 Bob Gibbons/WWI; p 119 Steve Teague; p 120 Bob Gibbons/WWI; p 122 Alan Watson/FL; p 123 Steve Teague; p 124 Bob Gibbons/WWI; p 125 *top:* John Robinson/WWI; *bottom:* G I Bernard/OSF; p 126 Steve Austin/WWI; p 127 Michael Leach/OSF; p 128 Deni Bown; p 129 Bob Gibbons/WWI; p 130, 131 Alan Watson/FL; p 133-5, 139, 141, 143, 148-9, 152-3 Gaia Books; p 136-7 Steve Teague; p 147, 151 Alan Watson/FL; p 154 Steve Teague.
Artwork on p 43 and p 44 by Mark Preston.

Danksagung

Gaia Books dankt folgenden Personen: Anne Brabyn, Tamsin Juggins, Patrick O'Halloran, und Deborah Pate für die Herausgabe und Recherche; Helena Petre fürs Korrekturlesen; Jenny und Owen Dixon für die Abbildungen; und Lynn Bresler fürs Korrekturlesen und den Index.

Register

9 heilende Öle …
9 Audiokassetten zur Untersützung damit Sie…
9 grundlegende Lebensaufgaben leichter lösen können:

Mit den Kassetten (nur in englischer Sprache) haben Sie die Möglichkeit diese Lebensaufgaben im eigenen Tempo zu lösen. Jeder Schritt wird leichter, wenn Sie das richtige Öl benutzen, das Ihnen die inneren Qualitäten bewußt macht, die Sie brauchen, um Prüfungen zu absolvieren, Probleme zu lösen und Ihren Weg zu gehen.

sich entspannen: ***Fichte***

ein Problem klarer sehen: ***Kiefer***

Selbstachtung aufbauen: ***Buche***

sich von der Vergangenheit lösen: ***Buchsbaum***

neu anfangen: ***Ginster***

eine Entscheidung treffen: ***Weißdorn***

sich motivieren: ***Walnußbaum***

Sie können die Kassetten und Öle
als Sets oder einzeln bestellen:
Cassetten (45 Minuten) je £ 8.75 + 35p Porto und Verpackung (in GB)
Öle (50 ml) je £ 7.75 + 50p Porto und Verpackung (in GB)
Auslandsporto bitte telefonisch erfragen
erhältlich bei
Gaia Books Ltd., 20 High Street, GB-Stroud, Glos GL5 1AZ
Tel.: +1453 752985 Fax: +1453 752987
E-Mail: Lyn@gaiabooks.co.uk

ebenfalls erhältlich bei:
Lieve Bonne, Ezelstraat 39, B-8000 Brugge
Tel./Fax: +3250 338754

Patrice Bouchardon steht für Workshops und Seminare auf der ganzen Welt zur Verfügung. Bitte setzen Sie sich mit Lyn Hemming bei Gaie Books oder mit Lieve Bonne in Verbindung.

Stichwortfinder

Zusätzliche Übungen mit Lösungen zu jedem Kapitel findest du auf unserer online-Lern-Plattform www.gute-noten-in.de

Mit deinem Passwort für Englisch, Klasse 7, kannst du dich ganz einfach kostenfrei einloggen und üben:

vb8D2z